# Getting Started in

# STOCK INVESTING AND TRADING

# Books in the *Getting Started In* Series

# Getting Started in

# STOCK INVESTING AND TRADING

## Michael C. Thomsett

WILEY

John Wiley & Sons, Inc.

Published by John Wiley & Sons, Inc., Hoboken, New Jersey.

Published simultaneously in Canada.

For general information on our other products and services or for technical support, please contact our
Customer Care Department within the United States at (800) 762-2974, outside the United States at (317)
572-3993 or fax (317) 572-4002.

Wiley also publishes its books in a variety of electronic formats. Some content that appears in print may not
be available in electronic books. For more information about Wiley products, visit our web site at www.
wiley.com.

*Library of Congress Cataloging-in-Publication Data:*

Thomsett, Michael C.
 Getting started in stock investing and trading / Michael C. Thomsett.
  p. cm. – (Getting started in..... ; 89)
 Includes index.
 ISBN 978-0-470-88077-7 (pbk); ISBN 978-0-470-93713-6 (ebk); ISBN 978-0-470-93714-3 (ebk);
 ISBN 978-1-118-03837-6 (ebk)
 1. Stocks–United States. 2. Investments–United States. I. Title.
 HG4910.T48 2011
 332.63'220973–dc22

                              2010028573

Printed in the United States of America

10 9 8 7 6 5 4 3 2 1

# Contents

## PART III

# COMBINING INVESTING AND TRADING

# Introduction

## The Potential of the Stock Market

In recent years, the stock market has been extremely volatile and many risks (and opportunities) were presented to investors and traders alike. Now more than ever before, it is essential for novice stock market investors to develop a complete understanding of the risks they face when money is placed in the market. This does not mean you should avoid investing; it does point out how important it is to become educated about risk in the stock market.

This book makes a distinction between investing and trading. An investor is an individual interested in identifying and buying shares of stock for long-term price appreciation, also called growth, and earning superior returns from dividends while protecting their capital. Part I of this book includes chapters about how to develop an investing program to build your portfolio based on the principles of fundamental analysis.

A trader, in comparison, is more interested in moving in and out of investment positions in the short term, making a higher volume of smaller profits. Traders rely on reading charts, spotting short-term trends, and taking advantage of the market's tendency to overreact to current news (meaning that the prices of stocks tend to move too far in one direction and then correct by reversing). This price swing is easy to spot in hindsight, but more difficult to anticipate ahead of time. Successful traders work on their skills in identifying the signs based on price charts. Part II is focused on trading skills and techniques, and is based on the principles of technical analysis.

The successful investor/trader learns how to combine the fundamental and technical analytical skills and uses both effectively. Mixing investment and trading speculation is a smart way to flexibly deal with a volatile and ever-changing market. Part III examines how this combined approach works.

The purpose in compiling this book is to present you with a range of valuable ideas, strategies, and market realities, all aimed at helping you to identify your appropriate risk tolerance level and then determine which investing and trading ideas are going to work best for you. Everyone is different, so no quick-fix or formula is going to work for everyone. In fact, trying to duplicate someone else's investing or trading system is not a wise idea because your unique profile (including income, assets, experience, and perceptions of markets and risks) demands that your approach make sense.

Today, many people are shy about the market. The volatility of recent years is a definite problem for anyone who puts capital at risk, but does that mean that staying out of the market makes sense? It does not. The alternatives are bleak. Savings rates are lower than ever before and do not outpace inflation. This means that even the modest inflation of recent years erodes the purchasing power of money left in savings. The only sensible alternative is to develop a program of investing and trading that minimizes risk while offering superior returns. Avoiding the market is just as great a problem as taking too many risks within the market; so the best approach is to develop a portfolio defensively.

A "defensively" built portfolio is one that is developed with complete knowledge about risk and opportunity, which you build and manage based on thorough research, acquired knowledge, and resistance of market forces. This book is designed with this necessity in mind. In the future, markets will go through cycles of relatively low volatility, followed by highly erratic months or even years. Investors and traders can earn profits in all kinds of markets, assuming that they have built a defensive portfolio and avoided taking risks they cannot afford. This makes it essential not only to understand risks, but also to define where you fit in the risk spectrum. Most people are going to be somewhere in the middle between extreme conservatism and extreme speculation, but that is a broad range. For this reason, both of the first two sections of the book begin with chapters examining and explaining a range of different risks.

The purpose in this endeavor is not to provide easy answers, but to help you to begin your journey into acquiring knowledge about a complex and changing stock market. Knowledge reduces risk and increases profit. This is the basic premise that has dominated the preparation of this book.

# Part 1

# Investing

# Chapter 1

# Investment Risks

Investing in stocks is an exciting, action-packed, fast-moving idea that for decades has excited many people—even those with little money to invest—with the possibility of building wealth.

It is possible to make money in stocks, but it is also possible to lose. The whole question of *risk*—exposure to losses due to a variety of causes—determines how slowly or quickly values change and which kinds of stock positions you end up taking. There are many industry sectors in the market, and each has its own risk characteristics. Some are especially sensitive to changes in interest rates, and others exist within a very specific market *cycle* of changes in profits.

Do you know the range of risks you face as an investor? Some people think that the sole risk they face is directly related to profitability. If you make a profit, you beat the risk; if you have a loss, you lose.

> **risk**
> exposure to loss resulting from numerous market, economic, and company-specific causes.

While this distinction is at the core of most investment plans, it is not the whole story. Every investor wants to earn a profit on every investment decision made. However, experienced investors also understand that it's a percentage game. You are going to have some losses along the way, and the key to succeeding is creating profits that are higher than the occasional loss, and for which the dollar amount is much greater.

## Key Point

No one is able to create profits in every instance. The key to success in the market is experiencing more profits than losses.

**cycle**
an economic tendency for sales volume and profits to change predictably due to economic or calendar timing. Among the best-known of market cycles is that experienced in the retail trade, which goes through specific seasons of high and low sales volume based on consumer buying habits.

This chapter examines a number of different risks every investor faces. It is not simply a matter of profits versus losses, but a more complex series of conflicts between supply and demand, timing, influences in and out of the market, and the economic climate. In other words, many things affect your portfolio and add to or take away from your spectrum of risk whenever you have money in the market.

# Market Risk

Most people understand the most obvious form of risk, known as *market risk*, or exposure to declining prices. This is only the first of many risks every investor faces and needs to manage.

Managing risk refers to how you structure your investments to maximize profits while minimizing the chances of losses. This requires careful selection of stocks based on sensible criteria, avoiding putting too much capital into any one stock, and continually monitoring the market to spot changing trends. It also requires that when considering any one company as a possible investment, you know what trends to examine and how to determine market risk based on the indicators you pick and track.

**market risk**
the risk that prices will decline, reducing the value of stocks, potentially for many months; market risk is the best-known and best-understood form of risk.

## Key Point

The purpose in setting up a portfolio wisely is not in completely avoiding risk, but in deciding how to manage it.

Will the value rise or fall? Realistically, you should understand that a stock's market value may either rise or fall. As apparent as this seems, some investors assume that their entry price is the "zero" point and that prices will rise from that level as soon as a buy trade is entered. This ignores the reality that prices can also fall. So managing market risk comes down to how well you select stocks and, equally important, how well you time the decision to buy. The better you are able to pick stocks appropriate for you and to determine when to buy *shares*, the less exposure you will have to market risk. The price changes are caused by many factors, but as a general rule, the concept of *supply and demand* determines the value of shares.

**shares**
part ownership of a corporation that is listed publicly. Shares are bought and sold over public exchanges. Owners of shares are entitled to receive dividends and common stock owners are allowed to vote on matters of corporate management. Shares of stock rise and fall in value every day based on the ever-changing levels of supply and demand.

Market risk is the ultimate expression of supply and demand. After you purchase shares, many changes can occur. If the demand for a company's shares is quite strong, prices will continue to rise; if demand is weak, prices might fall. When the supply and demand for shares are about equal, the price tends to stay within a narrow range. This condition, known as *consolidation*, is best described as a time of indecision. No one can tell whether buyers or sellers are in command and, as a result, it is impossible to predict whether the next price direction will be upward or downward.

Market risk is easily observed in hindsight. Everyone can see when they should have bought shares and, just as important, when they should have sold. For anyone interested in creating a long-term portfolio of profitable holdings, there are ten general guidelines for managing market risk:

1. Research a company before buying stock.

2. Look for changes after you buy shares.

3. Be aware of market cycles for the sector.

4. Know a company's position within the sector, remembering that the leader tends to outperform other companies.

5. Develop a list of criteria you consider most essential for narrowing down your choices.

6. Use past trends to predict how the future might look.

7. Give up some short-term opportunities gladly, in exchange for longer-term certainty.

8. Pick a wise plan and don't veer away from it.

9. Establish clear short-term and long-term goals and use these as guides for the decisions you make.

10. Never make a decision just because the majority is making the same decision; be a *contrarian* investor.

**supply and demand**
the economic forces that set prices for publicly traded stocks. When buyers want more shares than are immediately available from sellers, the excess demand drives up prices. When sellers want to sell more shares than buyers want to buy, the excess supply forces prices down. The interactive supply and demand forces are continuous.

**consolidation**
a period of indecision in the market, during which neither buyers nor sellers are in command. No one can determine whether prices will be driven higher or lower, so there is little or no movement during this time.

These are very preliminary suggestions that are expanded in coming chapters. However, the points above do provide you with an idea of how to pick stocks, which is at the heart of how you manage and reduce market risk.

---
**Key Point**

The more time spent in researching companies and their stocks, the better able you are to understand and manage risk.

---

# Leverage Risk

Among the many forms of risk, *leverage risk* poses one of the greatest threats to your financial health. This is the risk that arises when investors borrow money to buy stocks.

Most people will agree that it would be foolish to mortgage a home to the hilt to free up money to enter the stock market. The same people would not think it wise to seek a bank loan or line of credit to expand their portfolio. However, many of the same people will use a brokerage firm's *margin account* without hesitation. This is a form of borrowing. The margin account can be used to double up your positions. For example, if you have $20,000 to invest, you can take up positions as high as $40,000 under the rule that you have to maintain at least one-half of value in cash and securities. The rest can be borrowed in your margin account.

---
**Valuable Resource**

To review the rules governing margin trading and margin maintenance, go to www.sec.gov/investor/pubs/margin.htm.

---

A margin account is a great convenience, but using it increases your risk. If you expand a $20,000 to $40,000 and it earns

25 percent, you make a $10,000 profit. On only $20,000 in the same investment, you would earn only half of that, or $5,000. So the case for using leverage with a margin account is a strong one—until you consider what happens in cases of loss.

For example, if you start out with $20,000 in cash and borrow another $20,000 on margin, what happens if the $40,000 portfolio loses 25 percent? It falls to $30,000. Two things happen right away. First, your broker will issue a *margin call*, meaning you are required to meet minimum maintenance requirements, or keep 50 percent in the form of cash and securities.

In the example, the portfolio's overall value has fallen to $30,000 but $20,000 of that was borrowed in the margin account. So your capital value has fallen to only $10,000. The broker will issue a $10,000 margin call, meaning you have to bring your $10,000 of capital up to match the amount on margin, $20,000. If you cannot come up with the amount demanded by the margin call, your broker will sell off $10,000 of your holdings to pay down the margin. This results in a portfolio worth $20,000, half cash and half on margin. The net result: You have lost money, and your $20,000 portfolio now consists of $10,000 cash and $10,000 you owe to the broker.

**contrarian**
an investor or trader who makes decisions based on analysis rather than simply following the majority, and who recognizes that the majority is wrong more often than right, so making the opposite decision often is the smart move.

**leverage risk**
the risk resulting from borrowing money to invest. In the case of losses, leveraged positions not only have to be paid back, but losses have to be made up as well.

### Key Point

The convenience of a margin account is accompanied by the very high risk of margin investing. You might double your capital or lose it, all very quickly.

**margin account**
an account provided to investors by their brokers, allowing them to borrow up to one-half of the value of their portfolio.

The rule of thumb about borrowing money to invest applies to margin accounts as much as to any other form of borrowing. It is a great convenience and all too easy to use; but the risk is high if securities fall in value. This can occur very quickly and the risk is most severe when you are fully leveraged.

# Knowledge and Experience Risk

The second kind of risk involves the combination of two things: your *knowledge and experience risk* includes your investing background as well as the collective research you have performed for yourself in the past—performing online searches and studying books, magazine articles, or annual reports.

Knowledge should be acquired from sources that make sense to you. Today, especially with so many free online organizations providing free advice, it just makes sense to verify everything you discover (see Table 1.1). Sites that are selling something may offer claims that do not hold up. For example, if a web site wants you to subscribe to a service, make sure you know what you are going to get. If you are promised the "secrets of making millions" in the market or "things Wall Street doesn't want you to know," it probably involves a get-rich-quick scheme that is not going to work.

Market knowledge is best acquired when it is based on the recognition of what is truly needed to succeed in any endeavor. Success is the result of hard work, study, and analysis, but no one should rely on the claims by others to having knowledge as an easy and fast way to get rich. No one is going to sell knowledge to you. Most of us know all of this already, but it is also easy to fall victim to amazing promises for a one-time payment.

> **margin call**
> a requirement that investors deposit additional funds to meet minimum margin requirements. If the margin call cannot be met, the broker will sell some or all of the portfolio assets.

---

### Key Point

Never believe promises of systems that make it easy to get rich. You are never going to be able to buy fast profits. However, it is quite easy to waste your money on systems that don't work.

---

All of the knowledge you need is out there and it is just a matter of your deciding how to acquire it. You may ask friends and relatives who have been

---

### TABLE 1.1 Paper trading sites

*The following web sites offer free paper trading:*

| | |
|---|---|
| Wall Street Survivor | www.wallstreetsurvivor.com/home.aspx#1 |
| Investopedia | http://simulator.investopedia.com/Default.aspx?viewed=1 |
| Stock Paper Trading | www.stockpapertrading.com/ |
| Trading Simulation | www.tradingsimulation.com/ |

investing for many years which books or magazines to read, which web sites to visit, and how to gain solid, lasting information. You can also read reviews of books on Amazon.com or Barnes & Noble to identify the best books based on ratings and on what readers say about the books.

Experience, it has been said, often comes from making mistakes or losing money. If that is true, then losing a lot of money is "better" experience. This does not need to be the case. In fact, you can gain experience by *paper trading* stocks before actually putting cash on the line. Paper trading is a simulation involving real-time market price movement and the selection of stocks using a fictitious fund of cash.

A word of caution: Paper trading does not involve real money so the experience you gain is going to be limited. Just as you may acquire $40,000 playing blackjack on the free Yahoo! games site, when it comes to really putting $1,000 on a single hand, most conservative people will not do it. So by the same argument, don't deceive yourself into thinking that paper trading gives you real-world experience even though the decisions you make are going to be tracked based on the real market. At some point, you are going to need actual experience, meaning actual money will have to be invested in shares of stock.

Paper trading is an excellent way of learning the mechanics of trading stocks, finding out how margin borrowing works, and managing the payment and delivery of shares once an order has been entered. However, there is no substitute for the real thing. You can learn the theory of riding a bicycle by studying user manuals and watching films, but you do not actually learn until you get on the bicycle for real. The same is true for gaining investing experience.

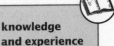

**knowledge and experience risk**
the combined information you have gathered through research and observation, plus past investing and related activities; together, knowledge and experience ultimately determines how you view the markets and how you approach selection of stocks.

**paper trading**
a system of simulated investing in which a portfolio of cash can be used to buy shares of stock based on actual value in the current stock market. However, because it is a simulation, there is no risk. The purpose of paper trading is to demonstrate to a new investor how the markets work.

## Key Point

Paper trading is a good way to become familiar with how the mechanics of investing work. But you can never appreciate the exposure to risk in the market until your money is on the line.

The risk associated with knowledge and experience is potentially quite high. If an investor makes decisions without understanding exactly what is taking place or how prices move, then the risk exists because of a lack of knowledge and experience. So the risk of making ill-informed decisions will lead to losses. Even worse, if a lucky but ill-informed decision results in a profit, an inexperienced investor may easily decide that it makes sense to place more money at risk, leading to large losses in the second or third trade.

**sector risk**
a risk identified with a particular sector and its industries, derived from business cycles, market conditions, or economic changes.

# Sector Risk

A "sector" is a segment of the market that is focused on one industry. Sectors include companies that share distinct product or service attributes or serve a particular market. (see Table 1.2)

The concept of *sector risk* relates to the cyclical and industrial risks each sector is vulnerable to or likely to suffer from in the event of economic conditions.

## TABLE 1.2 Sectors and industries

| Sector | Industries |
| --- | --- |
| Agriculture | farm and construction machinery; farm products |
| Banking | regional; foreign regional banks; money center banks; foreign money center banks |
| Basic materials | basic materials wholesale; packaging and containers; rubber and plastics |
| Capital goods | business equipment; industrial equipment and components; industrial electrical equipment; aerospace and defense products and services; aerospace and defense—major diversified; pollution and treatment controls; machine tools and accessories; fabrication; diversified machinery; small tools and accessories |
| Chemicals | specialty chemicals; chemicals—major diversified, agricultural chemicals; synthetics |
| Clothing | apparel stores; textile—apparel clothing; textile—apparel footwear and accessories; textile industrial |
| Communications conglomerates | diversified communications services; telecom services; domestic; telecom services—foreign; communications equipment; long distance carriers; wireless communications conglomerates |

## TABLE 1.2 (*Continued*)

| Sector | Industries |
|--------|-----------|
| Construction | heavy construction; residential construction; manufactured housing; general contractors; cement; lumber and wood production; building materials wholesale; general building materials |
| Consumer durables | home improvement stores; home furnishing stores; home furnishings and fixtures; appliances; housewares and accessories; photographic equipment and supplies; electronic equipment; jewelry stores; recreational vehicles |
| Consumer nondurables | food—major diversified; sporting goods stores; discount and variety stores; wholesale, other; toys and games; personal products; office supplies; cigarettes; specialty retail, other; grocery stores; department stores; sporting goods; recreational goods, other; cleaning products; paper and paper products |
| Credit | credit services; savings and loans |
| Drugs | drug stores; drugs wholesale; drug delivery; drugs—generic; drug manufacturers—major; drug manufacturers—other; drug related products |
| Electronics | electronics stores; diversified electronics; electronics wholesale; processing systems and products |
| Energy | oil and gas pipelines; oil and gas equipment and services; oil and gas drilling and exploration; major integrated oil and gas; independent oil and gas; oil and gas refining and marketing |
| Entertainment | toy and hobby stores; general entertainment; gaming activities; music and video stores; entertainment—diversified; resorts and casinos; movie production, theaters; restaurants |
| Food and beverage | food wholesale; specialty eateries; tobacco products, other; beverages—brewers; beverages—wineries and distillers; beverages—soft drinks; dairy products; processed and packaged goods; confectioners; meat products |
| Hardware | computer peripherals; computed based services; data storage devices; networking and communications devices; printed circuit boards; personal computers |
| Health care | specialized health-care services; home health care; medical practitioners; medical equipment and wholesale; medical instruments and supplies; biotechnology; health-care plans; health-care information services; medical appliances and equipment; diagnostic substances |
| Insurance | insurance brokers; surety and title insurance; life insurance; accident and health insurance; property and casualty insurance |
| Investing | closed-end fund—foreign; closed-end fund—domestic; closed-end fund—debt; diversified investments; investment brokerage—national; investment brokerage—regional; mortgage investment |

(*Continued*)

**TABLE 1.2 (*Continued*)**

| Sector | Industries |
| --- | --- |
| IT services | information and delivery services; Internet information providers; Internet service providers; Internet software and services; information technology services |
| Media | advertising agencies; CATV services; broadcasting—radio; broadcasting—TV; marketing services; publishing— periodicals; publishing—books; publishing—newspapers |
| Medical facilities | medical laboratories and research; long-term care facilities; hospitals |
| Metals and mining | nonmetallic mineral mining; industrial metals and minerals; aluminum; gold; copper; silver; steel and iron |
| Real estate | property management; real estate development; REIT—hotel and motel; REIT—office; REIT—residential; REIT; retail; REIT— health-care facilities; REIT—diversified |
| Services | lodging; waste management; personal services; sporting activities; business services; shipping; air delivery and freight; management services; security and protection; staffing and outsourcing; technical services; consumer services; catalog and mail order houses; education and training; research; all services, other |
| Software | application software; multimedia and graphics software; business software and services; technical and system software |
| Technology | scientific and technical instruments; semiconductor industries: equipment and material; specialized; broad line; integrated circuits; memory chips |
| Transportation | railroads; major airlines; regional airlines; trucking; trucks and other vehicles; auto manufacturers—major; auto dealerships; rental and leasing services; auto parts; auto parts stores; auto parts wholesale |
| Utilities | water; electric; gas; foreign; diversified |

Sector risk comes from the natural supply and demand cycle, economic conditions and their changes, political trends and actions, and perceptions among investors about specific sectors and industries.

# Political and Economic Risk

The risks associated with each sector and its industries are derived from many outside sources. Among these is *political and economic risk*, which are among the most important outside factors in assessing both the viability and value of a company, and identifying the timing of purchasing shares.

A closely related risk involves potential disruption of markets. So *disruption risk* may be a secondary fallout of either political or economic risk.

Examples of possible disruptions may include terrorist attacks that close down exchanges; power outages; catastrophic threats like pandemics, hurricanes, or flooding; or localized disruptions from labor strikes, regulatory enforcement actions, or even excessive price changes in the market. The exchanges employ stopgap measures on individual securities or even on the entire market if and when trading volatility exceeds specified levels.

**political and economic risk**
the risk that outside influences may affect stock valuation. Political changes, either domestic or international, may curtail activities or affect customers; economic activities may slow down production, prevent expansion, or prevent companies from hiring or retaining employees.

---

### Key Point

In cases of extreme price declines, exchanges will temporarily halt trading in a stock or, when the whole market is affected, on all stocks.

---

A trading disruption occurs in a specific security by way of a temporary suspension called a *trading halt* when news announcements that are pending are likely to create an imbalance. Examples include pending mergers or acquisitions, stock split announcements, or negotiations between companies concerning major news or consolidation or sell-off of major divisions.

A market-wide disruption can be put into motion automatically. The so-called *circuit breaker* is a programmed temporary suspension of all trading on exchanges due to exceptionally large price declines, or panics, threatening to create *liquidity risk* in the market. The halt may remain until the close of business for one session, or for a matter of hours only. The New York Stock Exchange (NYSE) identifies three possible circuit breakers at 10 percent, 20 percent, and 30 percent price declines.

**disruption risk**
the risk that trading in stocks may be disrupted by political or economic causes, acts of war, or natural disasters.

With the disruption risk in mind, especially when it develops to prevent loss of liquidity, a threat of lost liquidity—or liquidity risk—arises unexpectedly and poses a serious threat to an otherwise smoothly operating market system.

In some markets, liquidity is quite low and poses a different kind of threat. For example, in the limited partnership market, the lack of a secondary market

**trading halt**
the temporary
suspension
of trading in
a particular
security in
anticipation of an
imbalance that
may be created
by upcoming
announcements
of mergers or
acquisitions,
or negotiations
between
companies.

**circuit breaker**
an automatic
halt to trading
in all listed
securities on
exchanges,
triggered by
exceptionally
large price
declines and
set to last
a specified
number of hours
or until the end
of trading for the
session.

for units of partnerships may mean that investors wanting to sell will have to accept a deep discount. This occurs when there is no public auction market for those units. For publicly listed shares of stock, the exchanges are usually very liquid. Any shares of stock can be efficiently and easily bought and sold at the prevailing price. This transaction can occur at any time during the trading session and a growing market in after-hours trading extends not only trading, but liquidity as well.

# Inflation Risk and Tax Risk

Two forces—inflation and taxes—might not seem related but in fact, they are. And together they directly influence your investment profits. The first, *inflation risk*, is your exposure to higher prices. As inflation rises (meaning everything costs more money) your capital loses its *purchasing power*. This is a huge and eroding influence on your money. For example, to match the spending power of $100 in 1950, you would have needed $891 in 2009 just to match the purchasing power of that original $100.

| **Valuable Resource** |
| --- |
| To calculate the spending power of any amount between any two years, go to www.measuringworth.com/ppowerus. |

The effects of inflation are serious because as it rises, you need to earn a higher level of profits just to break even and maintain purchasing power. This translates to the demand for taking higher risks as a response to inflation.

If you are so adverse to market risk that you keep your money in a safe but low-yielding account, then you lose purchasing power. For example, in 2010 inflation was averaging about 2 percent. If you put your money into a certificate of deposit yielding only 0.75 percent over three months, you lose 1.25 percent of your money in reduction of purchasing power. You need to earn at least 2 percent just to match inflation—and that is before you consider the effect of taxes on your profits.

## Key Point

Inflation and taxes both reduce the value of your money; but together, they can have a severe effect on profits.

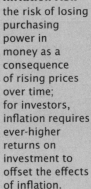

**liquidity risk** in the public exchanges, the possibility that high volume will curtail the availability of cash needed to complete trades in shares of stock.

Taxes come off the top of your earnings and only make it necessary to earn higher rates of return just to meet inflation. So *tax risk* is the threat that with part of your earnings going to federal and state income taxes, the remainder, or after-tax return, will not match inflation.

The tax burden is not only federal, but has to include the state tax liability as well. When both federal and state taxes are added together, the taxable percentage can rise as high as 50 percent or more.

**inflation risk** the risk of losing purchasing power in money as a consequence of rising prices over time; for investors, inflation requires ever-higher returns on investment to offset the effects of inflation.

## Valuable Resource

To find your applicable state income tax rate, go to www.taxfoundation.org/taxdata/show/228.html.

So both inflation and taxes play a part in identifying the scope of risk. To maintain after-inflation and after-tax purchasing power of your capital—without even considering a true net profit—you need to calculate the effects of both. Your *break-even rate* is the rate of return you need to make just to keep your purchasing power level.

To calculate the break-even rate, first estimate the rate of inflation you expect to experience over the next year. For this, you may refer to the federal web site for the Bureau of Labor Statistics (BLS), which calculates and publishes the Consumer Price Index (CPI), the usual measure of inflation.

**purchasing power** the value of money when compared between years. As inflation rises, the dollar loses its purchasing power compared to past years.

## Valuable Resource

To find the current rate of inflation, check the BLS web site at www.bls.gov/cpi.

**tax risk**
the risk that after-tax return on investment will fall short of the return needed to preserve spending power after inflation.

**break-even rate**
the rate of return needed from investing activity to absorb inflation and taxes, in order to maintain the purchasing power of investment capital.

**effective tax rate**
the rate of taxes assessed on taxable income, combining both federal and state rates.

The inflation rate is divided by the percentage of income remaining after you deduct the *effective tax rate* from 100. For example, if your combined federal and state tax effective tax rate is 44 percent, then the calculation involves deducting 44 percent from 100 percent; the answer is 56 percent.

When you divide the assumed inflation rate by the net percentage remaining after deducting your tax rate from 100 percent, the result is the return you need to earn to break even after inflation and taxes:

$$I \div (100 - E) = B$$

In this formula, $I$ is inflation; $E$ is effective tax rate; and $B$ is the break-even return. So if you assume a 2 percent tax rate over the coming year and your combined federal and state effective tax rate is 45 percent, your breakeven is:

$$2\% \div (100 - 44) = 3.6\%$$

This shows that you will need to earn 3.6 percent *net* on your portfolio to maintain your purchasing power. In "real" terms, earning this rate does not produce any real profits; it only maintains the value of your capital.

### Key Point

If you earn less than your break-even rate (after inflation and taxes), you are losing money on your investments. You will have to accept higher risks just to maintain your purchasing power.

With these assumptions, that 0.75 percent certificate of deposit is not going to be enough. You are losing purchasing power every year as long as you do not make at least the break-even rate. Table 1.3 summarizes the required break-even rate at various inflation rates and for different effective tax rate levels.

The higher your tax bracket and the higher the current rate of inflation, the more difficult it becomes to break even. This is the true meaning of the combined inflation and tax risk. It may be impossible to beat inflation

| TABLE 1.3 Break-even rate | | | | | |
|---|---|---|---|---|---|
| Tax Rate | 1% | 2% | 3% | 4% | 5% |
| 14% | 1.2% | 2.3% | 3.5% | 4.7% | 5.8% |
| 16 | 1.2 | 2.4 | 3.6 | 4.8 | 6.0 |
| 18 | 1.2 | 2.4 | 3.7 | 4.9 | 6.1 |
| 20 | 1.3 | 2.5 | 3.8 | 5.0 | 6.3 |
| 22 | 1.3 | 2.6 | 3.8 | 5.1 | 6.4 |
| 24 | 1.3% | 2.6% | 3.9% | 5.3% | 6.6% |
| 26 | 1.4 | 2.7 | 4.1 | 5.4 | 6.8 |
| 28 | 1.4 | 2.8 | 4.2 | 5.6 | 6.9 |
| 30 | 1.4 | 2.9 | 4.3 | 5.7 | 7.1 |
| 32 | 1.5 | 2.9 | 4.4 | 5.9 | 7.4 |
| 34 | 1.5% | 3.0% | 4.5% | 6.1% | 7.6% |
| 36 | 1.6 | 3.1 | 4.7 | 6.3 | 7.8 |
| 38 | 1.6 | 3.2 | 4.8 | 6.5 | 8.1 |
| 40 | 1.7 | 3.3 | 5.0 | 6.7 | 8.3 |
| 42 | 1.7 | 3.4 | 5.2 | 6.9 | 8.6 |
| 44 | 1.7% | 3.6% | 5.4% | 7.1% | 8.9% |
| 46 | 1.8 | 3.7 | 5.6 | 7.4 | 9.3 |
| 48 | 1.9 | 3.8 | 5.8 | 7.7 | 9.6 |
| 50 | 2.0 | 4.0 | 6.0 | 8.0 | 10.0 |
| 52 | 2.1 | 4.2 | 6.3 | 8.3 | 10.4 |

and taxes while also adhering to the market risk standards you set for yourself.

## Fundamental Risk

One form of risk that is not often discussed in risk terms is *fundamental risk*. This is the danger that the financial statements and reports issued by a corporation might be inaccurate and even deceptive.

Is this type of risk a serious one? In recent years, many investors have lost large amounts of capital due to intentional deception. The well-known case of Enron (among many other companies) involved not only

**fundamental risk**
the risk that financial reports on which investors rely may not be accurate and might even mislead investors in extreme cases.

intentional deception, but the willing participation of what should have been an independent auditing firm.

The rules governing how the numbers get reported are complex and allow companies leeway in how to interpret and report numbers. Financial results do not have any one interpretation, unfortunately, because many estimates are involved for setting up reserves, placing value on inventory, and the timing of when transactions are "recognized" (placed onto the books). Under the accrual accounting system, all income is supposed to be recognized in the year it is earned, even though cash may not change hands until the following year. All costs and expenses are supposed to be recognized in the year incurred, even if payment is not made until the following year.

---

### Key Point

Companies can and at times do distort their profit picture. Some distortions are legal under the accounting rules, so you need to track the trends over many years to get a grasp on the long-term growth curve.

---

This system is intended to ensure that the recognized revenue, costs, and expenses accurately reflect what happens each year. Because it is complex and involves estimates, it also lends itself to many liberal or aggressive decisions. Even worse, it is possible for companies to manipulate the reported outcome to make matters appear better than they are. This is what happened in Enron in the extreme.

There are many ways that companies can manipulate results, including:

- Exaggerating the current's year's revenues (reporting income that will not be earned until the following year).
- Deferring the current year's costs or expenses (setting these up as assets and then depreciating them over several years).
- Overvaluing or undervaluing inventory, bad debt reserves, and other accounting matters that have to be estimated.
- Delaying the reporting of one-time large losses.
- Changing the timing for recognition of the purchase or sale of a company or segment.

Some of these kinds of adjustments are not outright fraud but matters of interpretation. But there is a line between aggressive accounting and deception, and that line is not always easy to see in advance.

**Key Point**

It is very difficult to pin down the line between aggressive accounting and outright deception. It is only easy to spot in hindsight.

For investors who rely on the financial statements and earnings reports published by companies in order to make the decision to buy shares, the possibility that the basic information is not reliable is very troubling. The way to overcome this risk is to set standards for how you evaluate a company. These standards should include:

1. Check the numbers over as many as 10 years and look for consistent trends. When you cannot find those trends, investigate further.

2. Don't check only one or two indicators on the financial statements. Perform comprehensive analysis and compare trends in total rather than separately.

3. Consider the reputation of management as part of the equation of trust. Rely on management that has been around for a long time, in a company that has an impeccable reputation.

4. If something doesn't look right, don't ignore it. Rely on your instincts and question anything that looks out of line.

None of these four steps guarantees that you can always avoid fundamental risk. But as a general rule, if a company's stock is rising quickly and its revenue and profits continue to outpace the past year, a healthy degree of skepticism is in order. Outright fraud is rare, but aggressive accounting can be just as damaging even if it is legal. As long as everything continues to just get better, aggressive accounting is accepted by stockholders; but as soon as the market slows down, the more aggressively interpreted financial results tend to fall quickly as well.

## Lost Opportunity Risk

The final type of risk to be aware of is the risk that all of your capital will be tied up in positions and you will miss new opportunities as a result. The *lost opportunity risk* is a matter than virtually all investors face and have to make decisions to deal with or overcome.

**lost opportunity risk**
the risk that capital will be fully committed so that new investment opportunities cannot be taken, reducing future profits.

This risk comes about in several ways. In its most basic form, it exists whenever available capital is limited. Even if you employ your broker's margin account, if you cannot free up capital to invest in more positions than you hold right now, it is possible that many opportunities will come and go.

> ### Key Point
>
> You are always going to have to pass on most opportunities. The key to profitability is spotting a good opportunity when you have cash available to seize it.

A more severe form of lost opportunity risk occurs when you sell off holdings once they become profitable, but hold onto depreciated stocks. Of course, you hope those stocks will rebound and become profitable in the future; but when you take profits, you inevitably end up with a portfolio full of stocks that have fallen in value. A solution is to match up winners and losers. For example, if two of your holdings offset each other, sell them both and free up the total to invest elsewhere. If you have a profit of $3,000 in one position and a loss of $2,500 in another, by selling them both you free up more capital and you reduce your taxable income this year by offsetting profits and losses.

Risks are best managed by setting risk-related goals. Your *risk tolerance* has to define investments that are appropriate for you based on your experience, available capital, income, and perceptions about the market.

**risk tolerance**
the degree of risk appropriate to each individual based on experience and knowledge, available capital, income, and willingness or unwillingness to take chances.

If you do not want to risk loss, the defining phase of setting up your portfolio should be undertaken with one eye on the double effects of inflation and taxes. Settling for an exceptionally low return to avoid risk can easily lead to losses in terms of deterioration in purchasing power. It may be necessary to create a diversified risk to overcome the break-even level, but without accepting too much risk on your entire portfolio.

The next chapter expands on the discussion of how to select appropriate investments by exploring the concept of value for long-term growth of stocks in your portfolio.

# Chapter 2

# Value Investment

The way you select investments ultimately determines how successfully you will manage your portfolio and create future profits. The concept of *value investing* appeals to many people, especially the more conservative, because it bases decisions on analysis of the basic financial strength of a company, combined with the search for bargain prices of shares. This is the equivalent of buying a car by comparing ratings and performance, and then looking for an attractive discount. The alternative—buying a car based solely on its appearance—is a popular but less successful method.

> **value investing**
> a method for picking long-term investments by determining their true value and quality, and then seeking discounted prices to find bargains.

The alternative, based on predicting the future and then trying to find companies most likely to grow into the assumed scenario, *might* succeed but it is much less scientific than applying the principles of value investing. The technique of trying to anticipate the future is flawed in the sense that such assumptions are rarely accurate. It may also ignore or overlook some of the basic facts about a company's financial strength, competitive position, product or service trends, and economic forces that are going to affect future value.

### Key Point

Seeking investments conforming to assumptions about the future may ignore the basic facts about a company's strength or growth potential.

Those who try to pick investments based on assumptions about the future may actually outnumber value investors, whose emphasis is on analysis of financial fact rather than an attempt to predict future valuation and stock pricing. Value investing does not require you to predict the future or to be concerned with a variety of unknown influences on future prices. The decision to buy a particular company's stock is based on a study of current value, a history of growth, and application of a few sound fundamental principles (see Chapter 3). Returning to the analogy of the car buyer, a value investor goes to the dealership armed with comparative price and performance data, model comparisons and prices, and a very solid idea of the model and price desired. The decision is made ahead of time that if the price is available, they will buy; if that price is not available, they will wait.

The more impulsive car buyer goes to the dealership with little or no information other than what they might have heard about the brand. They end up buying for reasons that make no sense to the value investor. For example, they might buy a red car because it looks so nice...without considering the ratings, price, or performance issues.

For stock investors, the same principles apply. Value investors focus on individual companies, review the history of growth, read the annual reports, and decide in advance what is a fair price per share of the stock. It is simple and logical, but it requires more work. Once the true value of a company has been determined, the value investor will look for a buying opportunity. This means they will buy stock in the targeted company only if they can execute an order *below* the fair value price.

Do bargains arise in the market? Some theories claim that the current price of a share of stock is either efficient or random. (See Chapter 10.) An efficient price is one that has already factored in all known information about the company, meaning the price is always fair and accurate. A random price is one that changes without any prediction and may move up or down for reasons that cannot be known in advance.

### Key Point

If the market were either efficient or random, it would be a 50–50 proposition to ever buy stocks. Under those theories, the current price of stock is always "right" or "arbitrary."

Both of these theories are simply wrong. The market is anything but efficient. In fact, the inefficiencies of the market create may bargains. The "market" as one entity over reacts to all news, both good and bad, meaning prices tend to move too high on good news and fall too low on bad news. These jarring price changes tend to self-correct within a few trading sessions; but once they have fallen, bargains are created in a window of opportunity.

Few people accept the idea that the pricing of stocks is random. Many reject the principles followed by value investors, noting that financial information is always out of date by the time it is published. However, current news about products, earnings, and market perceptions all affect the value of stock very specifically. Rather than believing in the random approach to value, it makes more sense to recognize that there are many things affecting price, some canceling one another out and others confirming the current *trend*.

**trend**
the established direction or movement of price, or changes in an indicator, that define a company's value over many months or years.

Always remember the distinction between a technical trend (price movement) and a fundamental trend (changes in profitability, working capital, or financial strength). These are not the same, although they can be used together in analysis of companies and their stocks. However, even a consistent trend does not mean that *short-term* markets are efficient by any means. In the long term, a value investment is likely to be efficient in the sense that properly selected companies will experience growth. In the short term, however, the market is extremely inefficient and chaotic.

## Key Point

Short-term market trends are extremely random and chaotic. However, long-term trends rely on the fundamentals.

The theories concerning the efficiency of the market or its random nature are comforting to those looking at the market academically. But for people investing real money in shares of stock, these theories are either deceptively comforting (efficient at all times) or depressingly fatalistic (hopelessly random). Neither theory is realistic. The good news is that by applying the concepts of value investing, you can find value and a bargain price. It demands research and patience, but it is one way to build a profitable long-term portfolio. Two precepts every value investor has to be able to accept are:

**1.** Inactivity in a stock's price is not a negative attribute.

**2.** The market rewards patience.

It could take months, and in some cases years, for a stock's value to prove out the theory behind value investing. It is tempting to pay attention to the daily up-and-down changes in a stock's value, but that is not the way to preserve capital, avoid fast losses, or time decisions well. Value investors are patient and are willing to put in the time to research and analyze a company before buying shares.

# Value Investing and Control

Using the principles of value investing to select companies and their stocks is based on a few important rules:

- Base decisions on a study of the fundamentals (see Chapter 4). Anyone can grasp and master a few important fundamental indicators and trends.

- Compare companies to rank their quality.
- Be aware of price swings and *volatility*.
- Remember to include *dividend yield* in your analysis.
- Once you buy, don't worry about price changes; remember, the market rewards patience.

**volatility**
the degree of price change within a defined period of time, used as a measurement of market risk in a particular stock.

How many people truly buy stocks and manage their portfolios based on these simple but practical guidelines? Not many do, unfortunately. It is far more likely that investors, even those who define themselves as "fundamental" or "conservative" in their approach, tend to take the easier path of picking stocks impulsively. Someone tells a friend or relative, "You should buy this stock. It's going to double in value in the next six months." A common reaction is to immediately buy shares, but *without knowing why*.

**dividend yield**
the return on dividends paid. To compute the annual dividend yield, divide annual dividends per share by the current price per share; the result is expressed as a percentage.

| Key Point |
|---|
| Many investors buy stocks on advice from others, but may not know *why* that is supposed to be a good idea. |

An intelligent approach would be to respond with a question: "What criteria did you use to reach that conclusion?" In other words, *why* will the stock double in value and *how* do you know that? You will find that the person giving you the advice either has no criteria to rely upon, or has based the conclusion on a simplistic indicator. For example, the company has been growing at double-digit rates, it is about to introduce a new product, or it is going to benefit from new federal legislation. Those factors might influence stock value, but they do not guarantee anything.

Under the value investing approach, you have control when you apply the rules above and when you ask a series of your own questions:

- Is the stock currently fairly valued, overvalued, or undervalued?
- What criteria determine this conclusion about valuation?
- Is this company dominant in its industry?
- What is the recent price history and level of volatility?

Asking these questions puts you in control. Buying stock should be approached on the same basis as that used to buy a home. A diligent home shopper looks at many homes and compares prices and features. The decision should not be made rashly or without completely researching the local market, neighborhood, construction quality, and fairness of the price being asked. However, when buying stocks, the same careful homebuyers might make decisions impulsively and without any research at all. That is a mistake.

## Value Investing Myths and Facts

The power of value investing is in the control that people take over their own investment decisions. Rather than relying on unsupported claims or promises offered by others, or thinking of the market as a gamble, value investors are able to list out the reasons to buy stock, find companies meeting the requirements, and then act.

### Key Point

Value investing places full control in your hands; taking any other approach relinquishes control, either to someone else or to the luck of the draw.

There are a few myths and misconceptions about value investing worth examining and dispelling. These include:

- *Value investing is based on a study of fundamentals, and fundamentals are expensive and difficult to understand.* In fact, with the Internet now a dominant force in the market, a vast amount of valuable, free information is available to everyone. A little bit of study and research proves that using a few well-selected fundamental indicators is not complicated.

    Much of the information you need can be found in a company's annual report or quarterly financial statement, both of which are usually found on the corporate web site. All of the financial indicators you need can be found on a broker's free research links. For example, Charles Schwab & Co. gives its investors free access to the *S&P Stock Reports*, which are valuable sources for 10 years of fundamental information.

- *The key to value investing is getting stock at low prices.* This is not the case. The price itself is not the key; it is the price versus the value of the company. You would not want to overpay for a new home or for a car, and so you shop and compare prices. Value investors do the same thing with stocks. It is not the price per share that matters, but how that price compares to the true value of the company.

    A stock worth $15 per share could be overpriced based on an analysis of the fundamentals; and a stock priced at $80 per share could be a bargain. The price per share is a relative value, and value investing is not simply a matter of buying low-priced stocks.

- *The stock market cannot be beaten with any system, not even with value investing.* A pessimistic outlook is built from the way that people invest. If you take that "hot tip" and buy into a company without checking anything for yourself, you probably cannot beat the stock market. It is quite unlikely that a free hot tip is also going to work out profitably for you.

    In comparison, value investing is designed specifically to enable you to eliminate riskier choices, narrow down to a few stocks that meet your criteria, identify when you will sell as those criteria change, and make a decision based on analysis rather than on chance. With value investing, you have the best chance for beating the stock market.

- *Financial statements are too complicated unless you have a degree in finance or accounting.* The belief in the complexity of financial statements is true in one respect: To follow and interpret footnotes, especially those concerned with accounting valuations and highly technical matters, does require a great deal of expertise. However, for making investment decisions, you are going to be more concerned with *financial ratios* than with the details of the statements themselves.

- These ratios are found on the research services supplied by brokerages and, in fact, are not easily found on the financial statements. The 10-year summary of key financial indicators is of far greater interest than statements themselves, and much easier to find and use.

- *Growth stocks provide better returns than value stocks.* The popularity of *growth stocks* cannot be ignored. A growth stock is one expected to report earnings above the average of all stocks, which should translate to rapidly growing stock prices as well. Growth and value stocks have each prevailed in the market about equally. However, a danger in growth stocks is that they tend to outperform the market during big growth spurts, but to fall hard and fast when they end. The dot.com bubble was one such example of growth stock domination followed by a collapse. Over the long term, value stocks compete with growth stocks equally, but are less likely to crash.

**financial ratios**
tests of related financial data including operating results for a period of time (usually one full year), or the working capital and capitalization status as of a specified date (usually year-end).

**growth stocks**
stocks of companies expected to report better-than-average earnings and to experience rapid stock price growth as a result, at least for the period in which the growth industry remains in an uptrend.

# Setting Standards for Buying (and Selling)

With an impulsive method for buying stocks, you cannot know when to sell. By establishing a clear set of criteria for how and when to get in, you also can monitor those standards and, if and when they change, know when it is time to sell.

| Key Point |
| --- |
| Setting criteria for buying also defines criteria for selling. Without the first step, you cannot know when or why to sell. |

Value investors differ from all others in the sense that they set a number of important rules for how and when to buy. If the status of a company changes, the value investor is supposed to sell the stock. So it is a disciplined approach based on defining and seeking value and keeping the position as long as the company keeps meeting the criteria.

The selection criteria begin with an observation about the short-term and long-term market. In the short term, prices change based on company popularity, fads, rumors, and overreaction to all news. This chaos tells you that trading in and out of positions is a difficult game because you need to time decisions on both sides with near-perfect precision. The swings in price are not consistent, and the chaotic nature of the short-term market points to the importance of a long-term perspective.

In the long term, stock prices tend to move in line with the company's earnings. It's really that simple. If you want to identify a company that represents value, look to past earnings trends and determine whether those trends will continue into the future. Companies that see falling sales tend to also experience falling stock prices. For examples, check General Motors, Eastman Kodak, and any large U.S.-based airline from the 1990s through to today.

These four rather obvious (but often overlooked) facts point to the first criterion of value investing:

1. *Track earnings trends to find value companies.*

Another interesting fact about the market is that industries and companies experience popularity cycles. At certain times, the market is in love with one kind of company, whether that makes sense or not. At other times, the market ignores an entire industry. Value investors look for the company in an out-of-favor sector that has strong fundamentals but is not on many lists of "stocks to buy."

The reason for buying an out-of-favor company is that it is probably undervalued, but assuming the cyclical nature of most sectors and also assuming that the cycle will come around again, a second criterion for value investing is:

2. *Look for fundamentally strong companies in sectors that are currently out of favor in the market.*

The third rule is that you want to limit your short list to companies that have excellent reputations for quality of management, for product, and for competition. A value company is most likely to dominate its industry and has dominated for many years. By definition, this domination is the result of providing value products or services, and working through exceptionally skilled management.

The third value investing rule is:

**3.** *Narrow your list down to companies that offer exceptionally high-quality products or services, are managed expertly, and dominate their industry.*

A fourth market reality is that even if prices are set efficiently most of the time, there are times when prices are pushed downward to unreasonably low levels. A company's earnings might be lower than analysts expected, even if they represent record earnings for the company. It's irrational, but it is a fact of life. Bargains show up in the market all of the time because of the short-term irrationality of buyers and sellers.

With this in mind, you can look for bargain-priced stock when those prices fall in an exaggerated fashion. This assumes that you first qualify the company based on fundamental strength, exceptional quality, and competitive position within the company's sector. If you have done that, the fourth rule for value investing is:

**4.** *Identify companies you consider exceptionally well managed, that dominate their industries. Then buy on dips that create bargain stock price levels.*

These four standards come down to the central definition of value investing: the selection of stocks in exceptionally well-run companies, available at a price below fair value. The definition of fair value (at times also called intrinsic value) varies. In general, it refers to stocks priced below *tangible book value* or some other assumption of value based on fundamental analysis. This may also be affected by an exceptionally attractive dividend yield available at the time the purchase is made.

Value stocks tend to perform better than average during market downturns, either declining less than average or even rising. In 2007, when the DJIA lost 2,000 points, several value stocks (such as Altria, Coca-Cola, Exxon-Mobil, Merck, and McDonalds) rose in value. Even in 2008, one of the worst years on record, McDonalds rose in value while nearly all other stocks saw their prices decline.

> **tangible book value**
> the net capital value of a company (assets minus liabilities) further reduced for all intangible assets. When the tangible value is divided by outstanding shares of stock, the result is the tangible book value per share.

## Key Point

Growth stocks tend to climb rapidly, but also tend to fall just as quickly. Value stocks tend to accumulate value gradually over many years and in many market conditions.

In comparison, growth stocks tend to rise during volatile markets moving quickly to the upside. But there is a danger. Those same stocks tend to lose value rapidly when the uptrend ends, especially if it is driven by a temporary fad in the market dominated by those industries where growth stocks are found. Consider for example the cyclical rise and fall in technology and IT sector stocks.

This does not mean that value stocks insulate your portfolio from price declines. But well-selected value stocks do tend to out perform the market as a whole over the long term. Within that long term it is likely that some years will be low-volume and low-growth years for value stocks. However, as a rule, value investing is more conservative and more profitable than speculation or trying to find the next growth stock.

**reinvested dividends**
those dividends used to automatically purchase additional shares of stock as opposed to taking payments in cash. Reinvested dividends earn the dividend yield at a compounded rate because future dividend payments are based on the total shares held, including shares purchased with quarterly dividends.

A second source of returns on a portfolio, beyond price appreciation of stock, is dividend income. Most growth stocks do not pay dividends, so growth stock investors have to rely on price appreciation that outpaces not only the change in value investments, but their dividend yields as well. Value investors can make the most of dividend yield by reinvesting dividends in purchase of additional shares rather than taking payments in cash. The *reinvested dividends* appreciate at compounded rates. Over many years, dividend income on value investments represents a significant share of overall returns on the portfolio, and may also be thought of as offsets to the cyclical price declines that occur in all markets.

The value investor is probably more conservative and more concerned with volatility than growth investors. However, when your emphasis is on how a portfolio is going to perform over many years and not just over the next few weeks or months, value investing is likely to be a more profitable strategy in the market.

# Chapter 3

# Market Strategies

**E**very investor needs to develop a series of strategies for investing. An *investment strategy* is a set of rules and procedures you use to pick investments, decide when to close positions, and match desired returns with levels of risk.

Investing without a specified set of rules and procedures is not advisable. You need to know what is an acceptable risk and how you are going to manage that risk through a range of selections in your portfolio. Many novice investors focus only on finding stocks they believe will increase in value. The concept of investing in this approach is summarized in a single idea: Buy stock, wait for it to grow in value, and then sell.

**investment strategy**
a set of rules and procedures an investor develops for picking the elements of a portfolio, identifying desired rates of return and risk levels, and determining when to sell.

## Key Point

Finding stocks with appreciation potential is not enough. You also need to limit your search to stocks with acceptable levels of risk.

Of course everyone wants to make a profit. But without an investment strategy, how do you know which stocks to buy and which are too risky? How long will you hold stocks? What rate of return do you expect, or what dollar amount of profit will generate a sale? These are basic questions, but if you do not ask them, then you have not defined acceptable risks, appropriate stocks, or procedures for selling when the time is right.

## A Basic Strategy: Buy and Hold

The first and best-known market strategy is called *buy and hold*. Under this plan, you decide which stocks meet your risk criteria and are fundamentally sound, pay an attractive dividend, and are in a sector you believe has exceptional growth potential. You then buy shares of stock, intending to hold them for the long term. Properly selected value investments are likely to work best in a buy-and-hold strategy.

**buy and hold**
an investment strategy involving identification of value investments and purchase of shares, with the intention of holding those shares for the long term.

A buy-and-hold strategy may involve purchase of additional shares in the future, reinvestment of dividends, and well-planned diversification to avoid unnecessary market and cyclical risks.

If you combine the standards of value investing with a buy-and-hold strategy (often thought to be part of the same investment strategy), you will probably seek companies that pay a higher-than-average dividend, that are leaders in their sectors, and that have at least a 10-year record of exceptional performance under a short list of fundamental indicators (see Chapter 4).

### Key Point

Value companies share many attributes, including history of growing revenue and profits, higher-than-average dividends, and strong working capital controls.

Buy and hold tends to define an entire portfolio. Investors who are more conservative than average in their approach to portfolio management are likely to also be value investors. If you fit this definition, you probably will find yourself attracted to stocks that have a long history of outperforming not only the market in general, but other companies in their industry. This is one of the attributes of a value investment, and as part of the buy-and-hold approach, you are likely to be comfortable with the buy-and-hold approach to an exceptionally well-managed, competitive, and adequately capitalized company.

# A Strategic Requirement: Diversification

The idea behind *diversification* is that it does not make sense to place all of your capital in one place. The risk is too great. So you spread risks by selecting different stocks or other products, so that no single economic, cyclical, or market event or news will disrupt your entire portfolio.

> **diversification**
> spreading of risk among several dissimilar stocks or other investments, in order to avoid having a single risk event negatively affect the entire portfolio.

The methods of diversification are many. Best known among these is spreading risk by selecting different stocks. As a basic form of diversification, this move makes sense. Owning three stocks with equal dollar values in each, rather than placing all of your cash into a single stock, means that a decline in value of any one only affects one-third of the total.

## The Risk of Ineffective Diversification

This may not be enough diversification, however. If all three stocks are in the same industry, a change in the economy affecting that industry is also likely to affect all three stocks. Industries tend to share the same business cycles and to react to economic news (unemployment, interest rates, currency values) in a similar manner.

| **Key Point** |
| --- |
| Owning several stocks subject to the same kinds of market risks is not diversification; it is simply living with the same risks in different stocks. |

Even different industries may react to the same economic news in the same manner. So simply holding several different stocks might still expose you to market risk. For example, if you hold stock in three companies, all of which do the majority of their business overseas, how will currency exchange trends affect value? If all of your companies rely on borrowing money to fund operations, how will rising interest rates impact stock prices?

To truly diversify among different companies, your holdings should be among companies that do not share the same vulnerability, especially to factors likely to hit the stock price in a negative way. For example, if you buy shares in companies in different industries but all are technology stocks, any factors hurting stock prices are likely to lead to declines in the value of your entire portfolio.

## Diversifying by Company Size

**market capitalization**
the total dollar value of a company's net worth, including the most frequently used classifications of large cap, mid-cap, and small cap.

Another consideration in diversifying your portfolio is the level of *market capitalization* (market cap). This is a popular comparative measurement, representing the value of a corporation's *net worth* (assets minus liabilities). Net worth primarily consists of the value of capital stock and *retained earnings*.

Market capitalization is the sum of all outstanding common shares, multiplied by the current market price per share. So when stock prices rise, so does market cap; and when market price falls, so does market cap. The distinctions are made among companies not so much due to daily price fluctuations, but in broader terms. The three primary categories in terms of market cap are *large cap* ($10 billion or more of equity value), *mid-cap* (between $2 and $10 billion), and *small cap* (less than $2 billion).

Additional distinctions are made by some to include *mega-cap*, or companies whose net worth is greater than $200 billion; and *micro-cap*, including companies with equity value between $50 million and $300 million.

**net worth**
the dollar value of a company's equity value (assets less liabilities), divided into capital stock and retained earnings (the sum of all profits and losses from year to year) and other equity adjustments.

These distinctions are important because they provide an important method for diversifying beyond simply buying different stocks. The big-cap companies are often the strongest in terms of market domination. These companies also tend to fit the definition of *blue-chip* companies, those paying dividends even in soft markets, with stable and growing earnings and little or no long-term liabilities.

In selecting large-cap stocks, you opt for safety, but at times this may also mean lower-than-average volatility. Such companies at times, but not always, may move more slowly than the average company in the market. On the other end of the spectrum, small-cap stocks tend to be much more speculative because they are young and do not have a track record. However, those that succeed may do so with dramatic price appreciation. It's important to remember that every large-cap stock started out as a small-cap stock.

**retained earnings**
the accumulated sum of a corporation's after-tax net profits, increased each year a profit is reported, and reduced whenever a net loss occurs.

Market capitalization as a factor in diversifying is easily overlooked but can be one of the most important ways to spread risk. It's similar to buying real estate. Where do you buy? How much are houses worth? Is the neighborhood on the rise or on the decline? Are high-priced homes appreciating faster or slower than average-priced or low-priced homes? Anyone who tracks the real estate market understands quite well how the price range of homes defines market trends. The same is true for stocks.

## Key Point

Large, well-capitalized companies tend to be safer. They may also tend not to offer as much profit potential. Picking the right long-term investments is a balancing act.

**large cap**
a classification of companies whose total equity value is greater than $10 billion.

A method of diversification may be to spread capital among the three major classifications (large cap, mid-cap, and small cap) to expose yourself to potential price appreciation while also having a portion of the portfolio in safer companies with a longer track record.

The market is huge, and you will have no problem finding companies in any of the classifications. The total value of all publicly traded companies is about $40 to $50 trillion (Reuters, March 21, 2007; and Federation of Exchanges, www.world-exchanges.org).

**mid-cap**
a classification of companies whose total equity value is between $2 and $10 billion.

## Key Point

How much is a trillion? This amount is impossible to imagine. But some perspective helps. A stack of $100 bills adding up to $1 million is about five feet high. A stack equal to $1 billion is one mile. And a stack equal to $1 trillion is 10 miles high.

**small cap**
a classification of companies whose total equity value is less than $2 billion.

Diversifying by market cap is one of many ways to spread risk. An alternative to market cap is *enterprise value (EV)*, which is a measurement of the entire business, including both equity and debt capitalization. Market cap is based on valuation of *common stock* alone; EV adds *preferred stock* as well as all long-term debt.

You can also diversify in terms of liquidation risk, meaning buying some preferred shares to create an ultra-safe position for a part of your portfolio. You may also diversify by buying some domestic and some foreign stocks. Today, with the global online availability of trading, it is

**mega-cap**
companies with equity value above $200 billion.

**micro-cap**
companies with equity value between $50 and $300 million.

**blue chip**
companies with strong earnings, a history of regular dividend payments, and little or no long-term liabilities; financially strong and stable companies.

**enterprise value (EV)**
an alternative to the measurement of value based on equity alone, or market cap; EV includes all sources of capitalization, including holders of notes and bonds (debtors), as well as common and preferred stockholders.

easier than ever to invest around the world. Many specialized funds (see later in this chapter) also specialize by country or region. You can also diversify by investing in U.S. companies with a large share of income derived from overseas. Well-known examples include Johnson & Johnson (JNJ), Coca-Cola (KO), and McDonalds (MCD), among many others.

## Mutual Funds for Diversification

Diversifying by combining direct ownership of stock and other methods is a very popular choice. The *mutual fund* has been a widely popular investment vehicle for many decades. A fund is an organization that combines the capital of thousands of individuals to create a single diversified portfolio. Funds are organized by investment objective (conservative, aggressive), type of income (growth, income), or a balance of these criteria—an income fund, for example, focused on bonds and, to a degree, on stocks paying higher-than-average dividends. A balanced fund buys positions in both equity and debt.

### Key Point

Mutual funds can be found to suit any investment objective and type of investment. A study of performance in all kinds of markets is an important step in selecting a fund.

A variety of the traditional mutual fund is the *exchange-traded fund (ETF)*. This is a mutual fund that identifies a "basket of stocks" in advance and does not change that mix unless one of its components changes.

The traditional mutual fund can be bought and sold only by communicating directly with the fund's management. Value of a share of a mutual fund is determined at the end of the trading day only. In comparison, an ETF can be bought or sold on the public exchanges, and value changes during the trading day just like stock.

One great advantage to the ETF beyond its high liquidity is that it identifies its components in advance, meaning the management of the fund is virtually automatic. Mutual funds charge for managing a portfolio and once you buy shares you have little to say about the buy and sell decisions management makes. In an ETF, you know in advance what is in the fund. This is an advantage because it gives you automatic diversification; it is also a disadvantage because the return on an ETF is going to be the average of all its components. For example, if an ETF holds 10 stocks in one sector, of which three outperformed the others, the overall return is going to be equal to the average of all 10, not of the three outperformers.

ETFs exist for a variety of defined groups, including:

- Specific sectors or industries
- Stocks of specific countries or regions
- Shorts (ETFs that sell components instead of buying)
- Emerging markets
- Debt instruments, including fixed-income ETFs
- Currencies
- Real estate
- Commodities

**common stock**
(called "ordinary shares" in the UK) ownership in a corporation including voting rights for membership on boards of directors and corporate policies. Common stockholders have the lowest priority in the event of liquidation, below bondholders and preferred stockholders.

### Key Point

Exchange-traded funds are the hot new kind of mutual fund. They offer many advantages, but these are no guarantee that ETFs will always outperform the traditional fund.

**preferred stock**
classification of ownership with priority in dividend payments and liquidation above both debtors and common stockholders; however, preferred stockholders have no voting rights.

Every month, new ETFs are added to the growing list, and new categories are also added. The ETF market is an excellent way to diversify as long as you think the entire basket of stocks (or bonds) is worth holding. Remember, though, that an ETF will only earn the average return of all its components.

## Under- and Overdiversification

This brings up a new issue concerning diversification. Clearly, the best-known problem is *underdiversification*, a condition in which you are exposed to too

**mutual fund**
an investment company designed to combine the capital of many individuals to create a single portfolio designed to meet specified investment and risk objectives.

**exchange-traded fund (ETF)**
a type of mutual fund with a preidentified basket of stocks with a common element. The ETF is traded over public exchanges just like shares of stock.

much risk in your portfolio because your holdings are too similar and subject to the same market forces. Equally destructive is the opposite, or *overdiversification*, when you have capital spread out so broadly that overall returns are mediocre and, worst of all, below the market average.

If you overdiversify, meaning you spread your risks around to too many different stocks, you cannot beat the market average. This is a problem faced by mutual funds, especially very large funds. They are required to limit their holdings in any one company, so they have to buy many different stocks. As a result, many are overdiversified. As a consequence, most mutual funds report results lower than the popular indexes by which the markets are measured. Only one out of six funds performed better than the bull market of the 1990s (that's only 42 out of 258 managed equity funds examined). And the average margin by which those beat the averages was very slim. (These funds were measured against the well-known S&P 500 Index.)[1]

### Key Point

It surprises some people to hear that most mutual funds have done worse than the market averages. This happens for many reasons, among them the need to overdiversify.

A more recent study, from 2004 through 2008, revealed that 66.21 percent of all managed stock funds in the United States reported results worse than the overall market (measured against the S&P Composite 1500 Index).[2]

The overall report of 66.21 percent of all funds means that only about one-third of funds outperformed the overall market. This is due to overdiversification as one important factor in the outcome. In selecting a mutual fund for those who decide to choose that route, past performance is important but so is asset size.

---

[1] John C. Bogle, *Common Sense on Mutual Funds* (John Wiley & Sons, 2000)
[2] Justin Fox, "Breaking News: Mutual Fund Managers Keep Failing to Beat the Market," *Time/CNN*, April 20, 2009.

Diversifying with mutual funds might seem a logical and easy step. But be aware that smaller funds have greater flexibility than extremely large ones and can move money around more easily.

Buying funds is one way to diversify within the stock market. You can mix directly owned stocks with shares of mutual funds and ETFs. You can also mix between value investments and speculation, as well as stocks in between. Volatility levels is a sound test of market risk, so diversifying by levels of volatility is one final way to spread capital around.

**underdiversification**
a common condition in which a portfolio is focused on too few stocks or on stocks exposed to the same market risks.

## Other Market Strategies

Diversification dominates most discussions of market strategies. You need to spread risks while managing profits and losses, meaning constant monitoring and rethinking of past decisions. That is the nature of investing, and in uncertain markets, diversification is essential.

Beyond the need to spread risks, additional strategies can be very useful. Among these is *dollar cost averaging (DCA)*, a method of placing a fixed dollar amount into the market periodically. The theory behind DCA is that the averaging effect reduces risk and is beneficial over the long term.

Under this plan, you pay in the same amount each period (monthly, for example). If the price per share rises, you buy fewer shares; if it falls, you buy more shares. So you make three decisions with a DCA plan: the amount you invest, the frequency of transfers, and the overall time period over which the DCA plan will be made.

**overdiversification**
condition when a portfolio is spread so broadly that exceptional advantages in some holdings are offset by underperformance in others, resulting in a poor overall return.

**dollar cost averaging (DCA)**
a system of investing the same dollar amount into the market periodically regardless of price changes over time, on the theory that this reduces risk.

---

### Key Point

Dollar cost averaging is a formula for investing the same amount periodically. It is a strategy, and there is no guarantee that DCA investors will always make a profit.

---

A study of what happens if the stock price moves up or down shows how DCA has appeal to many people. For

### TABLE 3.1 Dollar cost averaging, rising market

| Month | Deposit | Share Price | Number of Shares | Average Price per Share |
|---|---|---|---|---|
| 1 | $500 | $20.00 | 25.00 | 20.00 |
| 2 | 500 | 20.50 | 24.39 | 20.25 |
| 3 | 500 | 22.00 | 22.73 | 20.83 |
| 4 | 500 | 22.25 | 22.47 | 21.19 |
| 5 | 500 | 24.00 | 20.83 | 21.75 |
| 6 | 500 | 25.00 | 20.00 | 22.29 |

example, if you transfer $500 per month into a stock currently selling at $20 per share, what happens if the stock price rises every month? An example is shown in Table 3.1.

Notice that as the price per share increases, the average price per share tracks the uptrend, but the average is always lower than the current market price. The proponents of DCA point to this as an advantage. There is also an advantage if and when prices fall as shown in Table 3.2.

When the share price falls, the average price per share falls as well, but is always higher than current market value. So if you had bought $3,000 of stock at $20 per share in a lump sum, it would get you 150 shares. At the end of the period, it would be worth $2,400, for a loss of $600. In comparison, the approximately 165 shares would be worth $2,719, for a loss of only $281. So in a falling market, DCA reduces the market risk.

To proponents of DCA, the proof is found in a demonstration of what happens in both kinds of markets. In a rising market, the basis is always lower than the current price. In a falling market, the loss is always less than it would have been buying a lump sum at the beginning of the period.

### TABLE 3.2 Dollar cost averaging, falling market

| Month | Deposit | Share Price | Number of Shares | Average Price per Share |
|---|---|---|---|---|
| 1 | $500 | $20.00 | 25.00 | 20.00 |
| 2 | 500 | 19.50 | 25.64 | 19.75 |
| 3 | 500 | 18.75 | 26.67 | 19.42 |
| 4 | 500 | 18.00 | 27.78 | 19.06 |
| 5 | 500 | 17.00 | 29.41 | 18.65 |
| 6 | 500 | 16.50 | 30.30 | 18.21 |

### Key Point

The decision to invest with DCA or by lump sum is a matter of personal choice, including opinions about how rapidly price appreciation (or decline) is likely to occur.

To critics of the system, the whole DCA looks like a gimmick. A variation is to time purchases of stock for price dips. Markets rarely move straight up or down over six months, but are more likely to experience price changes in either direction. So if you buy after a significant price decline, you get a better average price. For the long-term-minded value investor, the timing of purchases seems too much like a speculative timing strategy and may easily lead to lost opportunities if the price continues to rise while the investor waits on the sideline for the price dip that never arrives.

## Ex-Dividend Date Buying

Another strategy involves timing the purchase of stock right before the *ex-dividend date*. A stockholder has to own the stock prior to the closing of this date in order to earn a quarterly dividend, even though the dividend payment does not occur for up to a month later. So if you buy stock the day after ex-date, you will not earn a dividend until three months later.

This brings up an interesting timing strategy that even value investors can employ. For example, if a company has declared a dividend of $2.20 per share, every 100 shares earns $220 per year or $55 per quarter. If you buy 100 shares before ex-date, you are entitled to that $55. The price per share may dip on ex-date to allow for this benefit, but if you have also qualified the stock as a long-term value investment, it makes sense to time your purchase in this manner.

**ex-dividend date**
the cut-off date for earning of dividends. Stockholders who own stock before the close of the ex-date earn a dividend to be paid a few weeks later. Anyone buying stock after the ex-date has to wait until the next quarter before earning dividends.

### Key Point

Timing purchase with ex-dividend date in mind increases dividend income in the first quarter the position is owned.

Why wait three months before earning your first dividend when you could earn two quarterly dividends in the same time period? This doubles your dividend income in the first three months, just by being aware of the ex-date.

A related strategy is to reinvest dividends in the purchase of additional shares, which creates a compound return rather than a simple return based on dividend yield. Most brokerage accounts allow you to make this election at the time you purchase shares.

In all market strategies, you will also want to establish clear policies and goals for buying as well as for selling shares of stock. The basic goal of buying should be based on a complete analysis of a company's fundamentals (see next chapter). If you wait for a price dip to buy shares, you are likely to get a short-term bounce on the price, which is a good start to a long-term hold.

### Key Point

Knowing when to buy is an important skill. However, it is equally important to know when to sell.

It is equally important to know when to sell. Long-term buy-and-hold does not mean keeping a stock in your portfolio no matter what. Value investors need to continually monitor a company to ensure that it continues to meet the criteria for a value investment. As soon as a company's fundamental strength or profitability change, it is likely that stock prices will begin to decline. Recognizing the changes as soon as they begin gives you the chance to sell shares and find a new, stronger candidate. By monitoring the fundamental trends, you will be able to spot a reversal or leveling out of those trends, and to decide right away whether to continue holding or to sell.

The next chapter examines some of the more important fundamental indicators you need to track.

# Fundamental Analysis

There are two general schools of thought concerning how to pick stocks. This chapter examines the basic nature of *fundamental analysis*, the examination and analysis of *financial statements* and related news and trends, and how the indicators found in the historical record are used to pick companies and then buy their stock.

The second approach is technical analysis, or the analysis of price and chart patterns to spot reversals in trends and to time the purchase or sale of stock. The technical side is the focus of the second part of the book, and the specific indicators technicians use are found in Chapter 9.

**fundamental analysis**
the study of financial statements and the trends revealed in the numbers, to identify a company's revenue and earnings history and capital strength. The purpose is to identify companies representing the best investment value.

---

### Key Point

The most important difference between fundamental and technical is in the nature of data used. Fundamentals focus on the published results of operations; technicals involve price patterns and changes.

---

**financial statements**
summaries of a company's operations for a defined period of time (one year or the latest quarter), and of the values of assets, liabilities, and equity accounts as of a specific date.

**annual report**
a financial and marketing summary issued by corporations, including financial statements and detailed explanations, and management's interpretation of its financial and competitive position in the market.

On the fundamental side, the starting point of analysis of the most recent results of operations is found each year in the *annual report*. This not only summarizes the financial statements, but includes management's explanation of the financial record, markets, products, or services, and how the company plans to compete in the immediate future.

The annual report is available on the web site for a *listed company*. Most provide the report in either PDF or HTML format, or the report can be requested for delivery in hard copy. This is true for nearly all of the companies whose shares are traded publicly and owned by either *institutional investors* or *retail investors*.

The annual report is valuable because it includes extensive narrative sections explaining the significance of the numbers found in the financial statements. However, annual reports also have three major drawbacks for the purpose of performing in-depth analysis of trends:

1. *The statements and footnotes are very technical.* It is not easy to understand many of the technical accounting explanations included in the footnotes, which at times run 100 pages or more. The complexity of the accounting narratives makes annual reports useful to only a few financial experts.

2. *The narrative explanations may be factual or marketing-related.* It is not always easy to distinguish between factual interpretations of a company's results and the promotional spin management places on what may be a weak year or even a failed year. The management explanation is always upbeat and positive, making it difficult to determine how objectively the financial results are being interpreted.

3. *The annual report, in spite of its length, lacks detail.* To properly analyze the fundamentals, you need as many years of results as possible. Annual reports may provide only three or five years' worth of *selected* financial results, and in some cases only the current year and the previous year. Additionally, most annual reports leave out key ratios and indicators, so that you have to study the details to create your own base for analysis.

The drawbacks in annual reports are best overcome by relying on a longer-term summary of not only the key financial results, but the important indicators as well. Most online brokerage services provide members with free analytical services. One of the best of these is the S&P Stock Report, which is available for over 5,000 listed companies. This is provided free of charge to subscribers of Charles Schwab & Co., TD Waterhouse, Scottrade, and e*Trade. The S&P Stock Reports contain a wealth of information for a 10-year period. This includes not only the key information you find in the financial statements, but other valuable information as well for 10 years, including:

- Financial ratios derived from the financial statements
- Dividend history
- P/E high and low history
- Core earnings
- Extensive narrative analysis of the corporation and its markets

The *core earnings* deserve additional explanation. Under the rules accountants use, some nonrecurring transactions are allowed to be included in net earnings. However, Standard & Poor's developed a calculation to isolate the net profit from the company's "core" or primary business. The differences between net income and *core* net income can be substantial, so this is a valuable additional form of fundamental information.

**listed company**
a corporation whose shares are listed, quoted, and traded over a public exchange, with shares held publicly by either institutional or retail investors.

**institutional investors**
shareholders in publicly listed companies representing the majority of shares held, including mutual funds, pension programs, and insurance companies, as well as other concerns managing the investments of others.

**retail investors**
individuals who own shares in publicly traded companies through direct ownership (as opposed to buying shares in mutual funds).

**core earnings**
a calculated
adjustment to
net earnings
to isolate
earnings from
the company's
primary, or
core business.
All noncore,
nonrecurring,
or extraordinary
items are
adjusted out of
the calculation
of net earnings
allowed under
the accounting
rules.

---

### Key Point

Reported net income is not always the most
accurate summary of what took place for the
year. For that you need to track core earnings
and to be aware of the changes between net and
core—the bigger the changes, the less accurate
the traditional fundamental indicators.

---

Financial statements are prepared in a well-
defined but archaic format. This means that much of
the valuable information you need in order to track fundamental trends is simply not available from the latest
published financial statements or annual reports. This
is why you will find it more convenient to make use of
services like the S&P Stock Reports for 10 years of history, rather than trying to master financial statements
and how they work. However, it is also important for
every fundamental investor to know what financial statements contain and
what they reveal.

## The Balance Sheet

There are two kinds of financial statements and both follow a long-standing format of reporting. So if you understand how one set of financial statements is organized, you are well suited to follow any other corporate financial statement as well.

The first of these two is the *balance sheet*. It is given this name for two reasons.
First, it summarizes the ending balances of all asset, liability, and net worth accounts
as of a specific date. That date is the ending date of the period
being reported, usually the last day of the quarter or *fiscal
year*. Second, the sum of all asset account balances is equal to
the sum of liabilities plus net worth accounts.

**balance sheet**
a financial
statement
reporting the
balances of all
asset, liability,
and net worth
accounts as of
the last day of
the reporting
period.

The first component of the balance sheet is a category called *current assets*. These are all assets in the form
of cash or that are convertible to cash within 12 months.
Included are cash, accounts receivable, notes receivable,
marketable securities, and inventory.

In order, after current assets, the next group is called
*long-term assets* (also called "fixed assets"). This is the net
value of all *capital assets* minus *accumulated depreciation*.

After these two categories, additional asset groups include *prepaid assets, deferred assets,* and *intangible assets.* Prepays or deferrals are the values of expenses properly covering more than one year, and set up for annual *amortization* reducing the asset and transferring relevant portions to expense. Deferred assets are entire sums paid in advance but properly belonging to a future fiscal year. They are placed in the asset account until transferred to the expense category later. Intangible assets are all assets without physical value, including the assigned value of goodwill or covenants not to compete.

The asset accounts are added together to report the total of the corporation's properties, before being reduced by offsetting debts and obligations. It is important to use the subdivisions listed above, because so many ratios and indicators rely on distinctions between various asset classes.

**fiscal year**
the tax year used by a corporation, which may end in any quarter selected by the company. Fiscal years may correspond to the natural business cycle rather than to the calendar year.

---

### Key Point

The subcategories of financial statements are critically important. Many key ratios are based on isolated classes of accounts.

**current assets**
all assets in liquid form, meaning cash or convertible to cash within 12 months.

---

Assets are the top half of the balance sheet. On the bottom half are two main groups, liabilities and net worth. Liabilities include all of the debts and obligations (as well as any deferred credits), and net worth is the sum of capital stock, retained earnings, and other ownership accounts. Examples of "other" accounts include treasury stock, which is the value of corporate stock the company purchases on the open market and retires permanently.

**long-term assets**
the net value (basis minus accumulated depreciation) of capital assets, including real estate, autos and trucks, machinery and equipment, furniture and furnishings, and tools.

---

### Key Point

The total of all liabilities plus net worth accounts is *always* equal to the total of all assets, without exception.

---

The first group under the liabilities section is *current liabilities.* This is the sum of all debts payable within 12 months, including

**capital assets**
all assets set up
to be periodically
depreciated
because their
value outlasts a
single accounting
year; when fully
depreciated, the
capital asset's
book value is
zero.

**accumulated
depreciation**
the sum of
all years'
depreciation
expense
recorded and
claimed. The
annual expense
is offset by the
accumulation
account, which is
a negative asset,
or a reduction of
the book value of
capital assets.

**prepaid assets**
expenses paid
in one year
but properly
assigned to
two or more
years, set up
as an asset to
be amortized
properly to
future periods.

accounts and taxes payable and the current portion (12 months) of all long-term liabilities.

Next are the *long-term liabilities,* which are all debts owed by the company beyond the next 12 months. These include notes or contracts payable as well as the outstanding balances of bonds issued.

A final section included on this part of the balance sheet is not actually a liability, but a form of revenue received but not yet earned. All such *deferred credits* are assigned to this category. For example, a customer prepays a large purchase. The corporation has received the cash but it will not be earned until next year. In the current year, this is set up as a deferred credit.

The final section of the balance sheet is the net worth section. This includes capital stock and retained earnings as well as any other additional forms of net worth or adjustments. The sum of all net worth accounts is added to the sum of all liability accounts, and that total is identical to the sum of all asset accounts.

**Note:** How is the balance accomplished? The sum of liabilities and net worth is always equal to the value of all asset accounts because of double-entry bookkeeping. Every entry has a debit and a credit and these are equal in value. They may also be thought of as a plus and a minus. At any time, the sum of all accounts in the corporate books will add up to zero, because debits and credits offset one another.

## The Income Statement

The second type of financial statement is the *income statement* (also called "profit and loss statement" or "statement of operations"). This statement summarizes all revenue, costs, expenses, and profits for a specified period of time, such as a quarter or fiscal year.

### Key Point

Like the balance sheet, the income statement is divided into distinct sections. This is crucial for analysis as well as comparisons between companies.

The income statement can be easily summarized by its major parts and subtotals:

Revenue

    Minus: Cost of Goods Sold

Equals: Gross Profit

    Minus: General Expenses

Equals: Net Operating Profit

    Plus or Minus: Other Income and Expense

Equals: Pretax Profit

    Minus: Liability for Income Taxes

Equals: Net Profit

The category of *cost of goods sold* (also called direct costs) includes all expenditures that are assignable directly to revenue production, including merchandise purchased, manufacturing or production labor (direct labor), freight, and the net change in inventory levels for the year.

The cost of goods sold is expected to rise and fall along with revenue, and the percentage of these costs to revenue is expected to remain fairly constant. Changes may occur as a result of mergers and acquisitions, or disposal of an operating segment, when the mix of products also changes as a result.

When the cost of goods sold is subtracted from revenue, the resulting dollar value is called *gross profit*. Like the cost of goods sold, gross profit is expected to remain at about the same percentage level of revenue from year to year. This may change due to improved efficiencies, changes in inventory practices or valuation, and changes in market pricing.

Next, the expenses are deducted. These may be finely broken down into major groups such as selling expenses and general and administrative expenses (overhead), although most income statements show single values only and may explain the details through a footnote or supplementary schedule. When expenses are deducted from gross profit, the result is the *net operating profit*.

Next, "other" income and expenses are added or deducted. These include items such as currency exchange, one-time losses or adjustments, proceeds from the sale of capital assets, interest income or expenses, income from

**deferred assets**
expense payments made in one year but belonging completely to a future year, left as an asset until reversed and transferred in the proper accounting period.

**intangible assets**
assets lacking physical value, including goodwill and covenants not to compete.

**amortization**
the yearly amount of expense recorded and offset by a reduction to a prepaid asset account. For example, when a 36-month insurance premium is prepaid, it is amortized over the 36 months rather than reported as expense in the year paid.

**current liabilities** all debts payable within 12 months, including the current portion of long-term liabilities.

trading in derivatives, and all other nonoperating profit or loss. When the other income and expense net is added to or deducted from net operating profit, the result is called *pretax profit.* If other income exceeds other expense, the change will increase the net profit. If other expenses are greater, the change will decrease the net profit.

The final change is the liability for income taxes. This is deducted from the pretax profit to arrive at the final number, the *net profit* for the period.

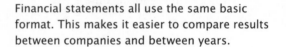

### Key Point

Financial statements all use the same basic format. This makes it easier to compare results between companies and between years.

**long-term liabilities** all debts of a company owed beyond the next 12 months, including notes, contracts, and bonds.

## The P/E Ratio: Finding a Bargain-Priced Stock

There are potentially dozens of indicators and ratios you can use to study the financial statements of a company. For the purpose of creating a basic starting point, focus here is on a very short list of fundamental indicators. These can be based strictly on the financial information you extract from the financial statements or, in one important exception, may combine financial and technical sides. This one exception is the *price/earnings ratio (P/E).* This is a comparison between the price per share and the reported *earnings per share (EPS)* reported most recently by the company.

**deferred credits** accounts in the liability section of the balance sheet, representing revenues received but not earned until a future period.

The P/E ratio is a good place to start in exploring a range of fundamental indicators because it combines technical (price) with fundamental (earnings), and also because it matches dissimilar timing indicators. Price is current, whereas earnings may be as much as three months in the past and not always reflective of what is going on today.

### Key Point

The P/E ratio combines technical (price) and fundamental (earnings) information to create a hybrid indicator.

Some analysts like to use *forward P/E* to analyze companies and their current earnings potential. This is a comparison between current price and estimated earnings for the coming year.

Justification for the forward P/E is that it makes the indicator more current. However, a lot of change can take place in the future, and as an indicator of stock value, forward P/E is not a reliable one. Any indicator that includes estimates should be used only cautiously.

**income statement**
a financial statement summarizing revenue, costs, earnings, and profits for a specified period of time, usually a quarter or fiscal year.

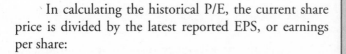

**Key Point**

The forward P/E is a difficult indicator to rely upon, because it uses estimates in place of published results. The historical P/E is more reliable, when studied over a 10-year period.

**cost of goods sold**
expenditures for merchandise, direct labor, freight, and the changes in inventory levels, all attributable directly to generation of revenue.

In calculating the historical P/E, the current share price is divided by the latest reported EPS, or earnings per share:

$$P \div E = P/E$$

For example, if the latest reported price per share is $42.50 and the latest reported EPS was $2.85 per share, P/E (rounded up) is:

$$\$4.250 \div \$2.85 = 15$$

**gross profit**
the dollar value remaining when the cost of goods sold, or direct costs, is subtracted from revenue.

This calculation applies to the current price. However, given the problem with timing of the two sides of the P/E, how can this ratio be used reliably to judge a company and its stock price? The real value in fundamental analysis requires long-term trend tracking, and the P/E is no exception to this. You need to find companies with a long record of the P/E remaining within what you consider a reasonable point range. For many, this is between 10 and 25, although opinions also vary. The higher the P/E, the more expensive the stock; that is the important thing to remember.

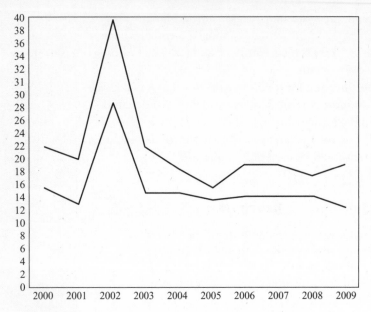

**FIGURE 4.1**   P/E ratio, 10 years: General Mills (GIS).

**net operating profit**
the dollar value remaining when all expenses are deducted from gross profit.

**pretax profit**
the net profit earned for a quarter or fiscal year, before calculating the liability for income taxes; the net left when other income and expenses are added to or subtracted from net operating profit.

Tracking the P/E range for a 10-year period demonstrates how the historical range of P/E from highest to lowest per year helps to find price and value stability. In Figure 4.1, the 10-year high and low P/E for General Mills (GIS) is summarized.

Notice how consistent the range has remained for the past seven of the 10 years. The high P/E never went above 21 and the low was consistently between 13 and 15. This demonstrates a very consistent record of fair pricing for General Mills' stock.

In comparison, the 10-year record for Caterpillar (CAT) paints a different story, as shown in Figure 4.2.

In this case, the five years in the middle of the range (between 2003 and 2008) were consistent and ranged between 17 and 12. However, as of 2009, the range exploded up to a high P/E of 43. This is troubling and indicates that at least at some point during the year 2009, Caterpillar was very overpriced. By April 2010 the P/E had moved even higher, to over 50. This does not mean Caterpillar was a poor choice as a long-term value investment, but with the P/E so high, waiting for a dip in price would make sense.

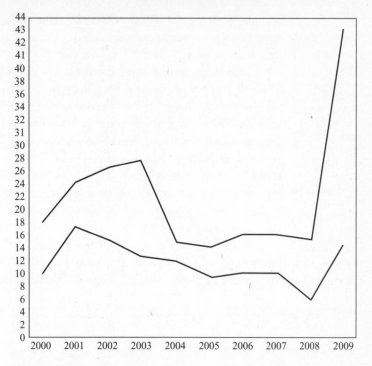

**FIGURE 4.2** P/E ratio, 10 years: Caterpillar (CAT).

**Key Point**

When you see a sudden upward spike in the P/E, it does not mean the company is a bad investment. It does mean the current price level is probably too high and may be due for a correction.

**net profit**
the "bottom line," the final profit when all adjustments and deductions have been made.

Tracking the P/E not in the moment but as a range over 10 years makes more sense, especially given the mix of technical and fundamental, and with the time disparity between current price and latest reported earnings.

## Revenue and Earnings: Fundamentals Based on the Operating Statement

The operating statement provides the second area worth detailed analysis over several years. Just as you cannot make sound judgments about the current P/E ratio

**price/earnings ratio (P/E)**

a comparison between the current price per share and the latest reported earnings per share, indicating the current market perception of future earnings potential.

without studying the longer-term trend, you cannot truly appreciate the significance of the current revenue and earnings without seeing how the trend has moved over a decade.

Tracking revenue and earnings is not just a matter of making sure that the numbers rise every year. You look for true growth, meaning that the dollar value of revenues and the dollar value of net earnings both rise each year. But you also want to see net profits maintained at a consistent or growing percentage of revenues. Even when the dollar value of earnings rises, if the percentage is declining, that is a negative sign. It probably means that costs and expenses are outpacing the growth in revenue, and that is never a positive trend.

Referring to the two previously cited companies as examples of the trend in P/E ratio, you can also track revenue and earnings trends over the same period. Figure 4.3 summarizes the

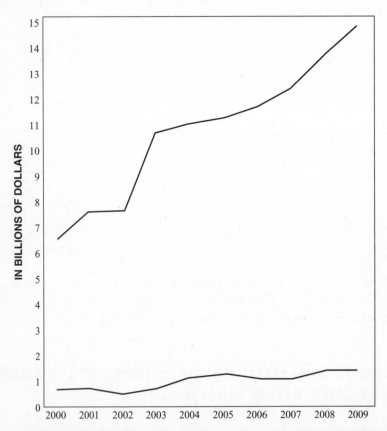

**FIGURE 4.3** Revenue and earnings, 10 years: General Mills (GIS).

General Mills (GIS) record of the operating results for a decade.

The dollar values of the revenue and earnings were very consistent in growing each year. The net return ranged between 9.0 percent at the earliest point to 8.8 percent at the latest year. The return spiked to 10.7 percent in 2005. However, the overall trend in revenue and earnings as well as net return was very consistent.

**earnings per share (EPS)**
the latest reported earnings, expressed as a division of earnings by the total shares outstanding during the reported year.

In comparison, Caterpillar experienced a steady improvement in net profits over the first eight years, a slight decline and then a huge drop in 2009. This occurred as the P/E shot up, as shown in the previous section. Figure 4.4 summarizes the revenue and earnings of Caterpillar over a decade.

Caterpillar's net return grew from 1.6 percent up to 8.7 percent in 2006, but the large drop in 2009 ended up with only a 2.8 percent net return. This kind of analysis, coupled with a study of the P/E range each year, helps to clarify the true condition of a company and its prospects for future growth.

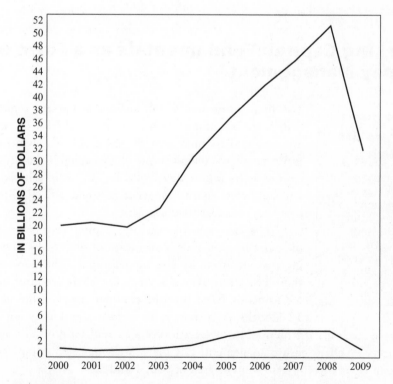

**FIGURE 4.4** Revenue and earnings, 10 years: Caterpillar (CAT).

**forward P/E**
a variation of
the P/E ratio in
which estimated
earnings for the
coming year are
used in place
of the latest
reported actual
earnings.

The study of revenue and earnings should track
not only the earnings and net return in relation to
sales, but also the gross profit and level of expenses.
This helps to determine the causes for deterioration in net return, although
the details are not always easy to find. You may need to rely on the details
in annual reports to discover the reasons for reduction in net return. Also be
aware that a change in the mix of products will affect the trend. Any time a
company adds an acquired competitor or sells off an operating segment, the
long-term trend should be restated. If it is not, then the trend is no longer
valid.

## Working Capital: Fundamentals as a Form of Money Management

**working capital**
the cash
available to the
organization
to pay current
obligations and
to fund future
growth and
pay dividends;
a fundamental
test of money
management.

The final major area worth analysis is *working capital.*
This is the amount of cash available to pay for current
expenses and to fund growth and dividend payments.
In its most basic definition, working capital is the net of
current assets minus current liabilities. But in a broader
sense, it refers to the longer-term trend reflecting the
company's management of cash.

The best-known working capital test is called
the *current ratio.* This is an indicator derived by dividing current assets by current liabilities. The outcome
should be a positive value, meaning there are most liquid assets on hand that the company owes in the next
12 months. A current ratio of less than 1 is a sign of
very weak cash management. The expectation of a current ratio of 2 or better means excellent cash management; but many well-managed companies
maintain their current ratio somewhere between 1 and 2.

The current ratio is rounded to a whole number and one decimal place. For example, if a company reports current assets of $1,462,000 and current liabilities of $845,400, the current ratio is:

$$\$1,462,000 \div \$845,400 .= 1.7$$

As with all fundamental tests, it makes sense to track current ratio for a full year. For example, in the case of General Mills and Caterpillar, current ratio over 10 years was:

**current ratio**
a popular test of working capital. Current assets are divided by current liabilities, and the answer is expressed as a single digit.

| Current ratio, 10 years | | |
|---|---|---|
| Year | GIS | CAT |
| 2000 | 0.5 | 1.5 |
| 2001 | 0.6 | 1.3 |
| 2002 | 0.6 | 1.3 |
| 2003 | 0.9 | 1.3 |
| 2004 | 1.2 | 1.3 |
| 2005 | 0.7 | 1.2 |
| 2006 | 0.5 | 1.2 |
| 2007 | 0.5 | 1.2 |
| 2008 | 0.8 | 1.2 |
| 2009 | 1.0 | 1.4 |

Both of these are consistent enough over time, although in the case of GIS, current ratio has often been below 1. However, the consistency in both companies is reassuring, if the analysis is limited to a study of only the current ratio. However, it is quite easy to manipulate this ratio by borrowing money and holding proceeds in cash. This raises the current asset level, but the offsetting liability is long-term and does not show up as a current liability (except the coming 12 months of debt service). This hides a potential problem: the rise of long-term debt. As long as the current ratio remains constant and is used as the sole test of working capital, this situation does not come to light.

**Key Point**

The current ratio is the best-known test of working capital, but it does not tell the whole story. The real long-term trend can only be understood by studying both current ratio and debt ratio.

**debt ratio**
an indicator derived by dividing long-term debt by total capitalization.

**total capitalization**
the combination of long-term debt (debt capitalization) and net worth (equity capitalization).

With this in mind, a second test is needed. The *debt ratio* is a comparison between long-term debt and *total capitalization*. The debt ratio is a percentage, but it is normally expressed as a value to one rounded decimal place, without percentage signs.

For example, a company reports current long-term debt of $41,200,000 and stockholder's equity of $98,600,000. Total capitalization is a combination of these two:

$$\$41,200,000 + \$98,600,000 = \$139,800,000$$

The debt ratio is found by dividing long-term debt by total capitalization. The debt ratio is:

$$\$41,200,000 \div \$139,800,000 = 29.5$$

This company is capitalized 29.5 percent by debt and 70.5 percent by equity. However, it is not the relative portion of debt or equity that is conclusive, since the levels of debt capitalization vary by industry. What is important is how the debt ratio changes over time. Whenever you see a growing debt ratio, it is a danger sign. The more long-term debt a company is obligated to repay, the worse future working capital will be. As a growing amount of annual earnings have to be paid to bondholders and note holders in interest, less is left for payment of dividends to stockholders or to fund future expansion.

An analysis of General Mills and Caterpillar for the 10-year period ending in 2009 shows how the debt ratio evolved.

| Debt ratio, 10 years | | |
|---|---|---|
| Year | GIS | CAT |
| 2000 | 94.7 | 66.9 |
| 2001 | 82.4 | 66.8 |
| 2002 | 57.5 | 67.9 |
| 2003 | 55.1 | 69.8 |
| 2004 | 50.3 | 68.0 |
| 2005 | 32.9 | 65.0 |
| 2006 | 21.7 | 72.0 |
| 2007 | 28.9 | 66.7 |
| 2008 | 35.4 | 77.2 |
| 2009 | 49.3 | 37.1 |

In the case of General Mills, the high debt ratio at the beginning of the period was troubling, especially considering that the current ratio was less than 1 for most of the period. However, the company cut its debt ratio by nearly one-half over the decade. Caterpillar, an industry in which high debt ratios are expected, maintained a consistent level with a sudden increase in 2008 and a surprising decline in 2009. However, the consistency of the company's current ratio, coupled with the debt ratio history, indicates sound cash flow management and healthy working capital.

| **Key Point** |
| --- |
| It is not the debt ratio in the current year that matters, but the long-term trend. When you see the debt ratio climbing every year, it spells trouble for future cash flow. |

In addition to determining whether to buy stock in any one company, you also need to determine whether it makes sense to own stock directly, or to rely on management of a mutual fund to build a portfolio and to buy shares in the overall holdings of that fund. The next chapter examines the role that mutual funds might play in your investment plan.

**Chapter**

# Alternatives: Stocks or Mutual Funds

For some investors, buying carefully picked stocks in well-managed, successful companies is a smart choice. As value investors, this route assumes that the important groundwork is done through analysis and comparison, and that the time is taken to understand not only the profit potential, but also the risk.

Buying stocks directly is not the only way to invest; however, many people who start out working with others or focusing on mutual funds eventually learn enough about the market that they feel comfortable buying stocks directly. It's a matter of personal choice and comfort, not to mention experience. A mutual fund is a *conduit investment,* meaning the fund's management handles portfolio decisions for its investors and passes through all profits in the form of dividends, interest, and capital gains. The fund acts as a conduit between the components of the portfolio and each investor.

## Investment Clubs

Some novice investors will eventually get to the point where they will feel safe buying stocks directly. However, that prospect can be daunting as well. For these individuals, some alternatives are available and can help not only to ease the apprehension, but also provide an education along the way. An *investment club* is a good place to start.

**investment club**
a group of
individuals
who pool their
money together
and share
research, to
select stocks for
purchase over a
period of time.

**open-end fund**
a type of mutual
fund that does
not place limits
on its number
of subscribers
or assets it
manages.

**closed-end fund**
a mutual fund
with a maximum
number
of shares
outstanding,
which trades
over a stock
exchange rather
than directly
between fund
management
and investors.
Market value of
shares rises or
falls based on
demand and
performance
rather than on
the market value
of the portfolio.

There are many ways to join or form an investment club. One of the best is to join the National Association of Investors Corporation, which supports over 8,600 investment clubs and has more than 90,000 individual members.

## Valuable Resource

The NAIC (www.betterinvesting.org) is an association of individuals belonging to investment clubs. They provide publications, forms, and advice from experts and fellow members.

Most clubs hold monthly meetings and members agree to deposit a fixed amount every month to pool together. At the meeting, the research shared by members is explained and discussed, and when appropriate the members decide which stocks to buy. Most clubs have about 15 members. Once club size moves above 20 or 25, it becomes difficult to keep the organization working smoothly and agreeing on a course of action.

## Key Point

Anyone apprehensive about picking stocks on their own will benefit by looking into investment clubs as a way to pool resources and capital.

A wise starting point is to agree among members and potential members on an investing philosophy and how research is to be shared. Most NAIC members subscribe to a conservative theory and rely almost exclusively on fundamental analysis of stocks to develop a list of investment candidates. If a club is to take greater risks or speculate in the market, all members should agree; otherwise this strategy will not be appropriate, especially for those new to investing.

## Key Point

Investment clubs work only if all members agree on the investing objective and appropriate risk level.

Investment clubs meet regularly every month, which is a good idea because it allows members to set aside the same time every month to attend meetings, and also lets people know how much time they have to complete their research before the next meeting date. The meeting is often held in a member's home, a local library, a church hall, or a coffee shop. The agenda for each meeting should be structured well, and should include updates on the portfolio's performance, research presentations by members, a talk by a guest speaker if available, and decisions about whether to invest in any additional stocks. The complete meeting should not exceed two hours at the most.

Since investment clubs pool members' money, they need to be set up with a formal organization and contract. NAIC provides valuable help in deciding which organizational form to use for an investment club. In addition, club members might want to pick a broker by referral and vote; or they might decide to be completely self-directed and use one of the many online discount brokerages.

Clubs generally need some form of organizational leadership as well. Clubs don't want to become overly formal, but electing officers and leaders of meetings just makes sense. At the very least, investment clubs need to elect a president or presiding partner, an assistant, a treasurer or financial manager, and a secretary or recorder.

Investment clubs can provide a good starting point for you. The shared research and acquired experience of 15 people is a powerful force, and it helps many people to gain knowledge and experience efficiently and profitably. For many others, mutual funds have been a popular choice for many decades.

**basket of stocks**
the preidentified, fixed portfolio in the exchange-traded fund (ETF).

**unit investment trust (UIT)**
a fund that purchases income-generating securities (bonds and stocks) and creates a trust in which shares are sold to investors. Periodic payments are made for interest, dividends, and capital gains earned throughout the life of the UIT.

# Types of Mutual Funds

**sales load**
a commission deducted from investments in mutual funds and paid to the salesperson.

The mutual fund industry is huge. There are thousands of choices for investors, and many different types of funds. These types are defined by investment objective as well as by the cost to invest. Objectives include growth or income, conservative versus speculative, and even type of investment. Some funds specialize in regions or countries, others in specific sectors or types of companies. Any theme you can imagine has probably been set up and organized in some type of mutual fund.

**load funds**
mutual funds that deduct a sales commission from all investments made, to be paid to a salesperson who recommends the investment.

| Key Point |
|---|
| Mutual funds are so popular that you can find one perfectly suited to your investment objectives. |

The basic type of mutual fund is an *open-end fund*, meaning that the fund will accept as many investors and as much money as it can raise, without limitation. So a successful fund is likely to grow over time as a growing number of new people open accounts and send in their dollars. This is the most common and popular type of mutual fund.

Compared to the open-end fund, the *closed-end fund* does place restrictions on the number of shares outstanding. While the open-end fund allows investors to buy and then redeem shares directly with the fund management, a closed-end fund is more like a stock. Shares are traded over a stock exchange and could actually grow in value above the true assets value of the portfolio, if demand for those shares is strong enough based on the fund's performance

There are few closed-end funds available today, and for every closed-end fund there are more than 13 open-end funds on the market. The newest type of mutual fund is the exchange-traded fund (ETF), which also trades on stock exchanges and contains a preidentified *basket of stocks* in its portfolio. In 1995, there were only two ETFs; by the end of 2008, there were more than 700 and the number expands rapidly every year.

A final broad classification in the mutual fund group is called a *unit investment trust (UIT)*. This is a type of fund that buys bonds and other income-generating securities, pools them together and then sells shares to investors. A UIT is not actively managed like a traditional mutual fund, because the portfolio of income securities is purchased in advance. Payments are made for capital gains, dividends, and interest as these are earned.

## Key Point

The ETF as an alternative to the traditional mutual fund makes sense; it is easily traded, management fees are minimal, and the portfolio is picked in advance.

**no-load funds**
mutual funds that are purchased without deduction of a sales load or commission.

The level of investment in mutual funds, ETFs, and UITs has grown substantially over the years. Table 5.1 summarizes the amount of cash placed into funds between 1995 and 2008.

The $10 trillion invested at the end of 2008 was owned by more than 93 million U.S. investors, according to the Investment Company Institute (ICI). The growth in mutual fund investing has been impressive.

## Valuable Resource

For more statistics and information about mutual funds, check the Investment Company Institute website at www.ici.org, and to see the complete annual Fact Book ICU publishes, go to www.icifactbook.org/pdf/2009_factbook.pdf.

### TABLE 5.1 Investments in mutual funds (in $ billions)

| Year | Open-End Funds | Closed-End Funds | ETFs | UITs | Total |
|------|----------------|------------------|------|------|-------|
| 1995 | $2,811 | $143 | $ 1 | $73 | $3,028 |
| 1996 | 3,526 | 147 | 2 | 72 | 3,747 |
| 1997 | 4,468 | 152 | 7 | 85 | 4,712 |
| 1998 | 5,525 | 156 | 16 | 94 | 5,791 |
| 1999 | 6,846 | 147 | 34 | 92 | 7,119 |
| 2000 | 6,965 | 143 | 66 | 74 | 7,248 |
| 2001 | 6,975 | 141 | 83 | 49 | 7,248 |
| 2002 | 6,390 | 159 | 102 | 36 | 6,687 |
| 2003 | 7,414 | 214 | 151 | 36 | 7,815 |
| 2004 | 8,107 | 254 | 228 | 37 | 8,626 |
| 2005 | 8,905 | 277 | 301 | 41 | 9,524 |
| 2006 | 10,397 | 298 | 423 | 50 | 11,167 |
| 2007 | 12,000 | 313 | 608 | 53 | 12,974 |
| 2008 | 9,601 | 188 | 531 | 29 | 10,349 |

*Sources:* Investment Company Institute and Strategic Insight Simfund.

| | | TABLE 5.2 Number of investment companies by type | | | |
|---|---|---|---|---|---|
| Year | Open-End Funds | Closed-End Funds | ETFs | UITs | Total |
| 1995 | 5,761 | 500 | 2 | 12,979 | 19,242 |
| 1996 | 6,293 | 498 | 19 | 11,764 | 18,574 |
| 1997 | 6,778 | 488 | 19 | 11,593 | 18,878 |
| 1998 | 7,489 | 492 | 29 | 10,966 | 18,976 |
| 1999 | 8,004 | 512 | 30 | 10,414 | 18,960 |
| 2000 | 8,371 | 482 | 80 | 10,072 | 19,005 |
| 2001 | 8,519 | 492 | 102 | 9,295 | 18,408 |
| 2002 | 8,512 | 545 | 113 | 8,303 | 17,473 |
| 2003 | 8,427 | 584 | 119 | 7,233 | 16,363 |
| 2004 | 8,419 | 619 | 152 | 6,499 | 15,689 |
| 2005 | 8,451 | 635 | 204 | 6,019 | 15,309 |
| 2006 | 8,723 | 647 | 359 | 5,907 | 15,636 |
| 2007 | 8,749 | 664 | 629 | 6,030 | 16,072 |
| 2008 | 8,889 | 646 | 743 | 5,984 | 16,262 |

*Sources:* Investment Company Institute and Strategic Insight Simfund.

The numbers of mutual fund companies by type is also interesting. Table 5.2 summarizes this information.

## Mutual Fund Fees

One of the biggest problems with picking a mutual fund is the variety and number of fees that might or might not be involved. The success of mutual fund investing has made it especially complex, and making valid comparisons is difficult. Some fees are hidden; some apply when you sell rather than when you buy; and some are given different names from one fund to another.

**front-end sales load**
an alternative name for the load, so called because a sales commission is deducted from an investment before funds are used to buy mutual fund shares.

### Key Point

Making like-kind comparisons among mutual funds is so difficult because the many different fees vary and are given different names.

The range of fees includes the *sales load*. This fee should apply only when you buy mutual fund shares through a broker or financial planner. As the name says, this is a sales commission paid to the salesperson who recommends a fund to you. A common fee is 8.5 percent, meaning that the minute you invest $100, the load of $8.50 is deducted and given to the salesperson.

The fee comes off the top, meaning that only $91.50 of your $100 goes into the investment. The group of funds known as *load funds* are those that deduct this commission. However, even if you purchase shares directly and without assistance from a financial planner, you might have this sales load deducted. Over history, there has been no trend of load funds outperforming the commission-free funds you can buy on your own, known as *no-load funds*.

A justification for paying a sales load *would* be that a financial planner has researched and compared all available funds and knows that the fund he or she is recommending is most likely to perform well in the market. This also assumes that the broker or planner has examined the portfolio and investment experience of management and has seen a clear distinction of one fund's performance over another. These assumptions are not necessarily true. The problem comes down to that commission. A salesperson who is compensated by commission is not going to recommend a no-load fund even if it is likely to outperform a comparable load fund. In addition, you should not assume that the research and comparison of investment value has even been performed before a recommendation is made.

**back-end sales load**
a variation of sales commission in a mutual fund, in which the commission is deducted when shares are redeemed, rather than when investments are made.

**contingent deferred sales load (CDSL)**
a back-end load, or sales commission assessed by mutual funds only if shares are redeemed before a specified number of years.

---

**Key Point**

If a financial expert is promoting a load fund as your best choice, ask for proof based on recent performance. Paying a sales commission does not ensure that you will be investing in a better choice.

---

**redemption fee**
a charge assessed by a mutual fund at the time that shares are redeemed, not to exceed 2 percent of the redemption value.

The load is also called a *front-end sales load* because the commission is deducted right off the top before your capital is invested in shares of the mutual fund. Recognizing how disadvantageous this is, some mutual funds have devised what is called a *back-end sales load*. This is a fee deducted when you redeem shares, so that

**management fee**
the fee charged
by a mutual fund
to compensate
its professional
managers.

**12b-1 fee**
a fee charged by
a mutual fund
for marketing
and promotion
to attract new
investors.

**prospectus**
a disclosure
document
explaining the
nature and risks
of securities,
including
management
and their
compensation,
investment
objectives, and
costs involved in
buying shares.

**shareholder
service fees**
a mutual fund's
charge for
expenses of
responding to
client inquiries,
either as part of
a 12b-1 fee or
separately from it.

the sales commission comes out of your accumulated investment plus earnings, rather than being taken before the investment is even made.

The back-end load may not be charged at all. In some very popular arrangements, the back-end load is actually called a *contingent deferred sales load (CDSL)*. This is charged only if you redeem shares within a specified period of time. If you hold shares beyond that deadline, the fee will not be assessed. The contingent load may be reduced over a period of years, eventually falling to zero for extended holding periods.

A mutual fund calling itself a "no-load" fund will not deduct a sales load, but many do assess other fees given a broad array of names. These include purchase fees, redemption fees, exchange fees, or account fees. None of these are considered sales loads as long as they do not exceed ¼ percent of the current value of an account. So a fund describing itself as no-load might change fees under a different name.

### Key Point

A fund called "no-load" is not always the cheapest to buy; a variety of fees and charges might apply.

A *redemption fee* differs from a back-end sales load in the sense that it is not paid to a salesperson, but is described as covering the cost the fund has to absorb when it redeems your shares. Redemption fees are limited to 2 percent or less of the value of redeemed shares.

All mutual funds charge some fees. These include the *management fee*, which is compensation for the professionals who research companies and make buy and sell decisions in the portfolio. The real test of a fund's value—whether load or no-load—is how effectively management makes its decisions and selects stocks or bonds to include in the portfolio.

Funds also assess numerous other fees, with descriptions like custodial expenses, legal and accounting expenses, or administrative expenses.

Finally, an important kind of fee that might be charged by either a load or no-load fund is called a *12b-1 fee*. Also called a distribution or service fee, this fee gets its name from the SEC rule permitting it (Rule 12b-1).

This rule allows a fund to charge a fee for advertising and marketing of the fund, including printing and mailing a fund *prospectus* to new potential investors.

So a 12b-1 fee is charged to current investors to raise money to attract new investors. This fee cannot be greater than ¾ of 1 percent of the fund's average net assets during the past year. Some funds mask fees intended for promotional activities by calling them *shareholder service fees*, which pay compensation to individuals who respond to shareholder inquiries or questions. This fee may be assessed separately or as part of a 12b-1 fee. If it is set aside separately, it cannot exceed ¼ of a percent of the fund's asset value.

**net asset value (NAV)**
the day's ending value of a mutual fund, computed by adding the total asset value of the fund (minus any liabilities) and dividing the net total by the number of shares outstanding.

### Key Point

The 12b-1 fee is charged to current investors to raise cash to market the fund to *new* investors.

The fee structure of mutual funds is confusing and often misleading, making side-by-side comparisons very difficult. With this in mind, you need to ensure that your comparisons between funds make true and accurate cost analyses as part of the effort.

**equity funds**
mutual funds that create a portfolio from investments in stocks (equities) of listed companies.

### Valuable Resource

You can compare fees, performance, and other facts about mutual funds by using a fund analyzer provided free of charge by the Financial Industry Regulatory Authority (FINRA). To use the analyzer, go to http://apps.finra.org/fundanalyzer/1/fa.aspx.

A second cost calculator, also free, is available at the Securities and Exchange Commission (SEC) website. Go to www.sec.gov/investor/tools/mfcc/holding-period.htm.

**fixed-income funds**
mutual funds that purchase bonds to generate interest income or stocks to yield higher-than-average dividends.

# Classification by Features

There are two additional considerations in the selection of funds. First is how fund shares are valued, and second is to understand the distinction between different kinds of mutual funds.

You will find daily listings for *net asset value (NAV)*. This is the ending day value of the fund's entire portfolio, divided by shares outstanding.

NAV is always calculated as of the day's closing prices. An ETF or closed-end fund, in comparison, changes in value throughout the trading day just like shares of stock that are publicly listed. This is most commonly used to track mutual fund performance. As NAV rises, it indicates positive results. And as it falls, it means negative outcome.

**balanced funds** mutual funds combining growth and income positions based on positions in stocks or combinations of stocks and bonds.

**specialty funds** mutual funds that select portfolios based on a specific theme, such as social consciousness.

---

### Key Point

NAV does not give you the best picture of relative value, because all current earnings are distributed in cash or reinvested to buy new shares; total annual return is a more reliable comparative measurement of fund performance.

---

However, NAV is not necessarily the best method for judging a fund's performance. Because a fund pays all of its capital gains, dividends, and interest to shareholders, different levels of current income will not be reflected in the reported NAV price. A more accurate measure is the fund's annual total return.

Performance is going to depend on the type of fund and how that classification performs in today's market. Of course, performance also varies based on management's selection of a portfolio and timing for its entry and exit decisions. There are nine major categories. These are:

**global fund** a type of mutual fund investing in companies outside of the United States or based in the United States but serving an international market.

1. *Equity funds* are the best-known ones. These invest in stocks. Because mutual funds are considered "institutional" investors, they trade in large blocks of stock compared to the relatively few shares traded by individuals, or retail investors.

2. *Fixed-income funds* (or "income funds") specialize in either bonds generating interest income, or stocks with exceptionally high dividends. These are both forms of income. Capital gains are also earned in these funds from selling stock above purchase price, or from redeeming bonds at face value when they were purchased at a discount.

**money market funds**
mutual funds that buy only short-term money market instruments, and provide income but no growth to investors.

3. *Balanced funds* combine potential growth from equity investments with potential income from dividends and interest.

4. *Specialty funds* are designed to pursue companies with specific features, in addition to defining themselves as equity, fixed-income, or balanced funds. An example is the "green fund" which includes only green technology companies in their portfolio. A *global fund* is another specialty fund that seeks positions in companies operating or based outside of the United States.

5. *Money market funds* invest only in instruments in the money market, which are interest-yielding and will not offer growth potential. These include certificates of deposit, U.S. Treasury bills, bankers' acceptances, and commercial paper.

**hedge funds**
companies usually set up as private partnerships and with a limited number of high-net-worth investors, specializing in high-return, high-risk leveraged market positions.

6. *Hedge funds* are not set up or regulated like any others in the fund universe. They are usually private partnerships that accept a limited number of investors and require a large deposit to participate. They use leverage through derivatives and other advanced techniques to create high returns (or high losses).

7. *Capitalization-based funds* specialize in companies of a specific market cap size. So there are large-cap, mid-cap, and small-cap funds suited for investors who believe the best returns will be found in one of those categories.

**capitalization-based funds**
mutual funds specializing in portfolios of companies based on market capitalization (large-cap, mid-cap, or small-cap).

8. *Index funds* do not buy stocks specifically, but invest in the broader market by tracking performance in an index like the S&P 500, the Dow Jones Industrial Average (DJIA), or other indexes that define and track market performance.

**index funds**
mutual funds that invest in market-tracking indexes rather than directly in equity or debt positions.

**tax-free bond funds**
mutual funds that invest solely in municipal bonds that offer tax-free interest to investors.

**mortgage pool**
a type of pooled investment in which shares consist of part ownership in a pool of secured mortgage contracts.

**Real Estate Mortgage Investment Conduit (REMIC)**
a mortgage pool offered by a government-sponsored or government-guaranteed mortgage organization.

**9.** *Tax-free bond funds* are similar to fixed-income funds in the sense that they take positions in bonds. However, this group buys only those bonds that are exempt from income tax. To determine whether such a fund is appropriate, investors should compare the after-tax return from the fixed-income fund to the tax-free return in this type of fund.

## Other Conduit Investments

In addition to mutual funds, there are many other ways to pool investments with others and within an organized structure, A *mortgage pool* is a mutual fund-like company that specializes in taking shares of a collection of mortgages. These mortgage-backed securities are offered by lending institutions sponsored or guaranteed by the U.S. government.

### Key Point

The widespread failure of mortgage pool–based investments in 2007–2009 proves that excessive risk invariably causes a strategy to fail.

These organizations include the Government National Mortgage Association (GNMA), also known as Ginnie Mae; the Federal National Mortgage Association (FNMA), or Fannie Mae, which also sells REMICs; and the Federal Home Loan Mortgage Corporation (FHLMC), or Freddie Mac. All of these market a mortgage-pool product called the *Real Estate Mortgage Investment Conduit (REMIC)*.

These mortgage pools have become controversial in recent years, due to excessive marketing and lax credit standards among participating lenders. Collectively, these organizations created a *secondary market* for real estate lending. Local institutions underwrote loans and then sold those loans to one of the big national groups, which then placed the mortgage into a pool with thousands of other loans and sold shares to investors. At least to some extent, excessive secondary market activity is what led to the housing bubble and crash of 2007–2009.

## Valuable Resource

To learn more about the secondary market for real estate and mortgage pools, check the websites for each of the three major organizations:

Ginnie Mae, www.ginniemae.gov
Fannie Mae, www.fanniemae.com
Freddie Mac, www.freddie.mac.com

**secondary market**
the government-sponsored market for purchasing of mortgage contracts from lenders, organizing them into larger mortgage pools, and selling shares to investors.

Another way to own real estate but have it act like stock is through the *Real Estate Investment Trust (REIT)*. This is a pooled investment that combines the money of thousands of investors to buy, construct, or develop real estate properties. REIT shares trade on public exchanges just like stocks, making them very liquid.

There are many types of conduits that specialize in all markets: stocks (equity), debt, and real estate. The right one depends on your own risk tolerance and personal investment goals.

**Real Estate Investment Trust (REIT)**
a real estate investment conduit that trades on public exchanges like shares of stock.

### Key Point

The REIT is a good way to invest in real estate but maintain liquidity and diversification.

# Variable Annuities

A final type of pooled investment is the *variable annuity*. This is similar in many ways to mutual funds, but with some equally important differences as well.

Variable annuities include either a lump-sum investment or periodic investments. An annuity, or series of payments, is guaranteed years later, but the amount varies based not only on how much is deposited, but also on how the portfolio performs.

### Key Point

Variable annuities are similar to mutual funds in many ways, but they are insurance products and involve many costs and fees.

**variable annuity**
a product similar
to a mutual fund,
which combines
investment
dollars from
many individuals
to create a
portfolio. The
issuing company
agrees to make
a series of
payments in
future years
based on
the value of
contributed
capital and
performance of
the securities in
the portfolio.

Because this is an insurance product and not like other investments, when you buy into a variable annuity, you are not an investor, but an annuitant. The future date when payments will begin is established in advance and is usually a specific age or retirement date. Within the variable annuity you are given a range of choices about where your money will be placed. These include a range of mutual funds, including splitting your money within one mutual fund company, but among a *family of funds* it offers.

Advantages that variable annuities offer over mutual funds include tax-deferred growth, a death benefit that goes to your beneficiaries and is equal to account value or a guaranteed minimum, and options for how you receive payments later (including a stream of payments for a guaranteed number of years, or guaranteed lifetime income, for example).

Disadvantages include a surrender fee if you withdraw funds early; expense fees that may be greater than comparable fees in mutual funds; and the overall complexity of the variable annuity contract when compared to buying shares in a mutual fund. Because most fees are not charged up front, variable annuities look like no-load funds. But fees are charged during the ownership period in the form of back-end penalties for withdrawal.

**family of funds**
a group of funds
offered by one
mutual fund
company but
with different
investment
objectives.

### Key Point

The best way to select any pooled investment is by ensuring that it matches your investment objectives, and that you completely understand what fees, risks, and requirements are involved.

Pooled investments—whether organized personally through an investment club, or more formally through a mutual fund, real estate pool, or variable annuity—are popular because they solve a familiar problem for a vast portion of the investing public. They automatically diversify investments, make reinvestment of income easy and automatic, and rely on professional management to make tough portfolio decisions.

The next section of this book discusses an alternative to investing, through various trading techniques. The distinction is made on three levels:

1. *Holding period:* Investment usually means a buy-and-hold strategy over many months or years; trading means moving in and out of positions in very short time spans, days or even hours.

2. *Risk level:* As a general rule, investors tend to be more conservative and traders more speculative in their market strategies.

3. *Source of information:* Investors are more likely to use fundamental analysis and to rely on financial statements and trends. Traders are more inclined to use technical analysis, study price charts, and time entry and exit based on price trends.

The many strategies used by traders are explained next, beginning with an analysis of trading risks.

# Part 2

# Trading

# Chapter 6

# Trading Risks

The first section of this book examined the range of techniques known as fundamental analysis, or the selection of companies based on financial strength and performance. In fundamental analysis, you examine the trends a company has reported to pick a logical and reliable investment.

In this section, the alternative—*technical analysis*—is described. Fundamental analysis relies on the most recent history of financial statements and the trends these reveal to pick companies. The technician analyzes price patterns and signs to pick a stock. These two approaches—picking a company based on history or picking a stock based on price patterns—are quite different. However, both fundamental and technical indicators can be used together.

The value of using fundamental and technical indicators together is that this provides you with twice the information. Both sources are worth studying, and neither is exclusively "right" or "wrong" for everyone.

Traders are understandably concerned with improving the timing of their trades. So they seek *entry and exit signals* in order to improve their timing. These involve a wide range of indicators that work together or, of equal value, contradict one another. Contradictory indicators should warn a trader away from making a

**technical analysis**
the study of price patterns, charts, and trends to time entry into and exit out of positions in stock, compared to fundamental analysis, which studies trends to pick companies.

**entry and exit
signals**
indicators
consisting of
price patterns
or changes,
which traders
use to improve
the timing of
buy and sell
decisions. These
signals are meant
to improve
their chances of
accurate timing
to increase
profits and
reduce losses.

decision merely because there is no clear or strong signal. Traders need reliable and consistent signs.

When you find a company that appears strong in all of the fundamental tests, the technical indicators can be used as *confirmation*, an independent and separate method for verifying the strength of a company as well as assuring yourself that your timing is good. The same confirmation action can work in the opposite direction, with fundamental strength confirming the strength of a stock and timing that technical tests reveal.

The first chapter of the previous section examined a series of risks from a fundamental perspective. The following sections take another look at the risk issue, but from a technical point of view.

**confirmation**
the use of
one indicator
to bolster or
support the
conclusions
reached by
what a different
indicator reveals.

---

### Key Point

Technical indicators are not only separate methods for timing entry and exit, but are also valuable as confirming signals for fundamentally based investment decisions.

---

## Market Risk and Volatility Risk

**investor**
an individual
most likely
to select
companies
based on
fundamental
strength and to
buy stock with
the intention of
holding it over
many months or
years.

The first distinction that has to be made between fundamental and technical analysis is that of risks. An *investor* is most likely to purchase shares of stock as part of a buy-and-hold strategy. This may last years or, for some, only a few months. The selection is based on the company rather than on the price trend in the stock. In comparison, a *trader* is more likely to focus on the price movement and trend in the stock and is much less interested in the fundamental strength of the company.

So investors focus on financial history and traders focus on current price. In summary, that is the most likely distinction between investors and traders; however, you can combine fundamental and technical analysis to round out your opinions of companies and their stocks, time your entry and exit, and diversify your portfolio. This also diversifies your risks, because the types and degrees of risk for investors and traders are not identical. They are quite different.

**trader**
an individual who buys and sells stock based on short-term price trends, who is focused on stock price changes rather than on the financial history of the company.

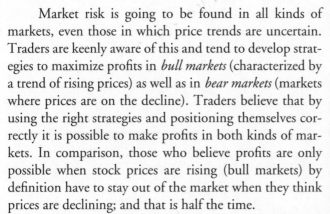

### Key Point

The basic difference between fundamental and technical is in focus, either on historical financial results, or on anticipating price movement.

Market risk is going to be found in all kinds of markets, even those in which price trends are uncertain. Traders are keenly aware of this and tend to develop strategies to maximize profits in *bull markets* (characterized by a trend of rising prices) as well as in *bear markets* (markets where prices are on the decline). Traders believe that by using the right strategies and positioning themselves correctly it is possible to make profits in both kinds of markets. In comparison, those who believe profits are only possible when stock prices are rising (bull markets) by definition have to stay out of the market when they think prices are declining; and that is half the time.

**bull markets**
markets characterized by generally rising prices of stocks over a period of months or years.

Market risk was explained in the first chapter and from a fundamental perspective. A fundamental investor (likely as well to be conservative) has to be aware of price volatility even though the selection criteria include mostly or exclusively a range of fundamental indicators. Most fundamental investors seek stocks of companies with exceptional capital and market strength that are likely to rise in value traders rely on technical indicators (and are more likely to be drawn toward *speculation* rather than a buy-and-hold strategy), and they understand that

**bear markets**
markets of declining price trends over a period of months or years.

price volatility defines risk. So market risk from a fundamental point of view can be clarified and called *volatility risk* for the technical trader. Traders are likely to recognize the potential for profit in either bull or bear markets, and also are likely to use a range of different strategies that work in both situations.

Volatility risk is specifically related to the *breadth* of the *trading range*. This is simply the point spread between the most recent high and low price levels at which a stock has traded. Breadth is relative, however. In a $10 stock, a breadth of two points is considerable; in a $100 stock, it is less volatile simply because the stock's price is higher. So breadth defines volatility, and the degree of breadth is the price movement in comparison to the price level of the stock.

**speculation**
short-term trading based on price movement in order to maximize profits based on immediate price movements and trends, distinguished from investment, which tends to involve longer-term hold periods.

**volatility risk**
a technical variation on the broader market risk, involving the degree of exposure traders accept in picking and timing positions in stock.

**breadth**
the span of price movement within the current trading range, representing the number of points of movement over time.

The trading range can be thought of as a reflection of supply and demand, just as it works in any other market. In real estate, if houses within one neighborhood usually sell for between $135,000 and $150,000, the "trading range" of housing is defined between those high and low prices; and the "breadth" is $15,000. This could also be called a 10 percent breadth, because the price difference between high and low is 10 percent of the high.

In the stock market, breadth and trading range are what define volatility risk. The greater the breadth, the greater the risk. For traders, who are most likely to focus on short-term price movement, higher volatility means greater profit potential in a short period of time. It also means greater volatility risk. For most traders, the most realistic approach is to focus on the stocks with moderate volatility, thus accepting moderate volatility risk in exchange for potential profits. If volatility is too high based on a self-defined risk tolerance, the stock is not appropriate. If volatility is too low, then traders will be equally disinterested because in exchange for low risks, profits are also unlikely.

### Key Point

The trading range is the entire framework for technical analysis, and for identifying varying levels of price volatility. Virtually all technical indicators rely on observations of price movement in relation to the trading range.

Trading range, or the price difference between high and low trading in recent sessions, is the most important technical concept to remember. Without identifying a trading range, you cannot interpret current price movement or identify risk levels.

In technical analysis, two terms are essential, as they frame the trading range and give meaning to the current supply and demand for shares of a particular company. These are *support* and *resistance*. Support is the lowest price in the trading range, or the lowest level at which sellers and buyers can strike an agreement to exchange shares. Resistance is the highest point in the trading range, or the highest level where price agreement is possible under prevailing conditions.

The concepts of support and resistance define the majority of technical indicators, and traders rely on the structure provided by the trading range (defined as the price breadth existing between support and resistance) to identify strength or weakness of price movement. Most technical indicators involve price "tests" of support or resistance. A *breakout* below support or above resistance has significance, whether it represents creation of a revised trading range, or fails and price then retreats back to the established trading range. Many indicators involve failed tests of these borders, often preceding price movement in the opposite direction.

**trading range**
the distance between recent high and low price levels; the price area in which buyers and sellers currently interact with one another.

---

### Key Point

The borders of the trading range—support and resistance—are the "lines in the sand" that identify success or failure of all short-term price movement.

---

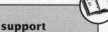

**support**
the lowest price in a stock's trading range, or the low side of the price range at which sellers and buyers are able to agree on price.

The trading range, its breadth, and the action between price and the borders of support and resistance are the entire structure of technical analysis. Trading relies on interpretation of price patterns and, specifically, on how price moves within (or breaks out of) the support and resistance borders.

**resistance**
the highest price in a stock's trading range, or the high side of the price range at which both sides can agree to a trade.

## Leverage Risk

Traders also face the endless challenge of how to make the best use of capital, based on their risk tolerance and willingness to use borrowed funds. Investors have to contend with this as well. Do they limit investments to available cash or use margin accounts to virtually double their potential positions? The more leveraged a position, the more profit potential *and* the greater the risk of loss.

**breakout**
price movement
below support or
above resistance,
signifying
creation of a new
trading range or
a failed attempt
in which prices
retreat back to
the established
trading range.

For traders, leverage is just as much of an issue. However, because traders tend (generally) to be willing to assume higher levels of risk than investors, their leverage risk may be greater as well. With more potential for loss, leverage may mean much greater dollar value to loss as well as dollar value to potential profit. This is a reality for traders, and as a consequence many will limit their use of basic tools such as margin accounts simply to keep risks low even in trading strategies demanding greater risk levels. So the overall risk should be part of the equation for traders; greater risks associated with short-term trading can be made even greater by also maximizing the use of a margin account, for example.

---

### Key Point

Leverage is a great way to double or triple your profits; it is also an efficient way to expand your losses just as quickly.

---

To keep this in perspective, ask yourself: Would you max out a homeowners' equity line of credit (HELOC) to free up funds to trade stocks? Most people would reject this as too high-risk and also as an action likely to threaten the security of their home. However, the same people who would deem using home equity too risky might use a margin account to double up their positions in stocks. If the stocks lose market value, the money borrowed in a margin account has to be repaid.

For example, assume you have $20,000 in cash. Under the margin rules, you have to maintain 50 percent in cash and securities, meaning you can borrow $20,000 in your margin account and create stock positions of up to $40,000. If the prices of stocks go up 20 percent, the $40,000 placed into shares of stock increases in value to $48,000. The $8,000 profit is great, and is twice what you would have profited using only cash. However, what happens if the positions lose 20 percent? Now the account is valued at only $32,000. Because you have to maintain that 50 percent value in your margin account, you would get a margin call from your broker, and would be required to either come up with another $8,000 or sell some of your holdings. The $8,000 would restore value to $40,000 and satisfy the 50 percent margin requirement. If you do not meet the margin call, your broker then sells $8,000 of your holdings. This reduces your account value to $24,000 and also reduces your margin to $12,000.

Leverage risk for traders based on maximum margin can be described as the risk of losing twice as much in exchange for the potential of gaining twice as much. Before creating maximum margin positions, it is important to understand this risk and to be willing to accept it or, if not, to avoid margin trading altogether.

### Key Point

Margin-based investing is simply getting access to the potential for doubling profits...or losses.

Another way that traders use leverage is through the use of *options* in addition to buying and selling shares of stock. Options are intangible contracts to buy or sell lots of 100 shares of stock. They cost only a fraction of what it would cost to trade 100 shares, and that is where options are so attractive and have become popular as a trading and speculative tool.

**options**
intangible contracts allowing their holders to control 100 shares of a specific stock for a fraction of the cost of trading those shares.

Options are attractive not only as speculative tools, but also as a means for managing a portfolio. For long-term investors, options can provide insurance for paper profits, or create short-term profits for no added market risk. However, they are complex instruments and are more completely explained in the third section of this book.

For the moment, it is only necessary to understand that options are excellent leverage products. However, they involve specific types of risk. Your brokerage firm will allow you to trade options only once you have established your experience in options trading and knowledge of risks. You also need to maintain a level of account value in order to trade options, which requires a margin account; and brokerage firms require minimum account value before the margin account is available.

Brokerage firms assign trading levels for options trading. Under the lowest level, you are allowed only the most basic of trading techniques. More than any other method of trading, options are complex in terms of the jargon and sheer number of possible strategies. Some are very high-risk and others are quite conservative. Remember, however, that as with all kinds of strategies, knowing the range of risk is the essential first test you need to pass before placing money into the market. This applies to options and other forms of leverage more than with the act of just buying stock.

# Short Position Risk

**long position**
ownership
of shares,
accomplished
by a buy order
and involving the
sequence buy-
hold-sell.

Traders can take up two general kinds of positions in the market, whether involved with stocks, options, or exchange-traded funds (ETFs). The best known of these two is a *long position*. Under this approach, you buy shares of stock or an ETF (or an option contract). The sequence of events is the well-known buy-hold-sell.

Traders can also take up the opposite approach, the *short position*. Under this approach, you sell shares (or options) as a first step. This exposes you to substantially higher market risks.

**short position**
the sale
of shares,
accomplished
with an opening
sell order and
involving the
sequence sell-
hold-buy.

For most traders, the long position is better known whether it involves all cash or margin (or other forms of leverage). Traders who use short positions generally take much greater risks. So *short position risk* describes using the initial sale to create profits when the value of the stock falls, or involves the risk of loss if and when the value rises.

Short positions are used in a variety of different ways. Selling stock, a strategy called *short selling*, is a complex and potentially high-risk strategy. Under this approach, your brokerage firm borrows the shares of stock and lends them to you to sell. So you have to pay interest on the borrowed stock while also being exposed to market risk. You hope the price of stock will fall so you can close the position at a profit. If the price rises, the transaction ends up in a loss.

**short position
risk**
the risk incurred
by selling as an
opening step,
in which traders
hope for a price
decline so the
short position
can be closed
(bought), and the
net difference
will be a profit.

Most people new to trading will be likely to avoid short selling as an acceptable strategy. The risk level and cost of shorting stock are too high for most individuals; and with the use of options, it is possible to play a bear market without needing to go short.

# Extreme Reaction Risk

Imagine mortgaging your house to get all the money you could, selling everything else you own, and converting all your assets into speculating on the price of a single tulip bulb.

As insane as that sounds, it happened in the 17th century, not just to one person but to a spectrum of people from all walks of life. This famous example of a market mania has been called the "tulip mania" and it had a disastrous outcome. The prices of tulip bulbs exchanged as commodities ran up to unbelievable levels when speculation fever took over and thousands of people wanted to get in on the amazing profits. The rarity of tulip bulbs was the beginning of the problem. A seed may require 5 to 10 years to produce a tulip flower and another 3 to 5 years to work itself into a bulb. Rarity is also defined by specific color markings. In 1635, the commodity trading activity began on tulips still in the ground, and the action was done via promissory notes instead of the exchange of cash. Trading even went beyond this, with sales made for tulips that had not yet been planted. This was called a *windhandel* (wind trade).

> **short selling**
> the act of borrowing stock and then selling it in the hope that the price will fall. If that occurs, shares can be closed by buying at a lower price. If the stock price rises, it creates a loss because the short position has to be closed (bought) at a higher price. Short sellers also have to pay interest on the shares borrowed to open the short position.

---

### Key Point

As irrational as the tulip mania was, it was not an isolated case of temporary insanity. Trading in all markets is always susceptible to manias of exactly the same kind.

---

Prices ran up very quickly, within less than one year, and one record-level sale involved the sale of 40 bulbs for 100,000 florin. To put this in perspective, a *ton* of butter was worth 100 florin at that time. Two years after it began, the bubble reached its peak and very quickly evaporated. Thousands of speculators, mortgaged and leveraged to the hilt, were completely destroyed practically overnight.

This puzzling event took place on a large scale and involved commodity prices running into outrageously high price levels. It relied on a true mania, a form of greed in which those on the outside think they are losing the opportunity to get rich like everyone else. They take risks they cannot really afford and get into the market, and the new demand creates even higher prices.

There are three issues that define greed buying like this. First, when profits look easy or automatic, logic is abandoned. People will pay anything just to get a position in the market as long as they are sure prices will keep rising. Second, speculators think the upward move will never end. And third, speculators do not set exit levels for themselves, where they will take their profits and get out. Oddly, when asked, speculators express the belief that they will somehow just know when prices are peaking. The truth is that as long as there is someone else willing to pay more, speculation looks like a game impossible to lose. But the day finally arrives when the new speculators run out. The "greater fool theory"—the belief that there are always plenty of people who will pay more than you did—only works for a while.

---

### Key Point

Greed trumps logic; it also trumps risk awareness and ultimately destroys a speculator's plan to double up and get out.

---

The same mentality works when markets are falling. Panic is just as irrational as greed, and traders will sell out of positions to avoid bigger losses tomorrow. The result of greed and fear is that traders may buy high and sell low instead of taking the sage advice to "buy low and sell high."

The *greed and panic risk*—or *extreme reaction risk*—can be expressed in another way: "Bulls can make money, and bears can make money. Pigs and chickens get slaughtered."

**greed and panic risk**
the risk that buying will occur irrationally when prices are running up too far and too fast, or that selling will occur when prices are falling rapidly.

Tulip mania was not just an oddity that happened once 400 years ago. Similar manias have occurred throughout the history of trading in stocks and commodities, even quite recently. Between 1995 and 2000, the dot.com bubble that created the new Internet sector at one time had thousands of companies selling stock, many of which produced no products and offered no services. As many inexperienced first-time entrepreneurs became millionaires overnight based on nothing but a public offering, a growing number of others jumped onto the trend. Today, many of the most successful companies are survivors of the dot.com years, but for every success story there are hundreds of cases of people losing everything, not only in start-up offerings, but also in speculation in the stock of these new companies that have nothing in the way of assets or even products.

**extreme reaction risk**
the risk that timing of buying or selling decisions will be based on overreaction to market conditions rather than rationally based or based on observed technical signals.

---

### Key Point

The dot.com fad of recent history was just as illogical as any other mania. Traders invested fortunes in companies with no tangible assets and no product or service. It's no surprise that most of the dot.com companies are no longer around.

---

At various times in the history of the United States, investment crazes have occurred in real estate, cotton, railroads, canals, the auto industry, time-share computers, and biotechnology, to name only a few industries. In most of these instances, the few companies that survived produced a product that had a market, but often with too many players. For example, in 1910 there were more than 200 auto manufacturers selling cars in the United States.

## Technical Knowledge and Experience Risk

In Chapter 1, knowledge and experience risk for fundamental investors was analyzed and explained. This referred to the actual investing background an individual needs to have before being able to realistically understand the stock market and how it works.

**volume**
the level of trading in a stock, represented by the number of shares exchanged between buyers and sellers in a specified period of time (a trading day, for example).

Of equal importance is a variation of the same idea, or *technical knowledge and experience risk.* This is quite different than the fundamental risk requiring an understanding of financial statements and trends. On the technical side is the range of price and *volume* trends and measurements of price movement. This includes a lot of formulation and the study of how different moving averages converge or diverge; how subtle shifts in price patterns or *gaps* in between trading sessions change the picture and anticipate what comes next. The name "technical" analysis is accurate because it is very technical and in many instances difficult to grasp.

The need for a keenly developed interpretive skill cannot be emphasized too much. Technical analysis is focused primarily on price trends or, more to the point, on anticipating price direction based on the most recent indicators. Many of these are hard to spot or can be misread; even the best-understood technical signal can also turn out to be a *failed signal,* meaning that an indicated

**gaps**
spaces in trading found between one session's close and the next session's open.

direction simply does not materialize. Technicians attempt to manage or spot failed signals by confirming what appears to be going on or by waiting for a secondary change in the current trend.

The technician who relies on the study of price indicators is also called a *chartist* because he or she studies price charts of selected stocks in the attempt to spot entry and exit signals, and to make a move before the larger market also recognizes what is going on. A chartist who succeeds in the early detection of

**technical knowledge and experience risk** the risk that a range of technical indicators is difficult to explain without a background in interpreting them and recognizing their significance and effect on price trends.

developing price changes is probably more experienced than the average trader, and knows how to interpret signals as well as spot a potential failed signal.

# Technical Risk and Market Culture

Technical analysts are different kinds of people than fundamental analysts. Technicians enjoy the fast-paced action of the moment and are probably more willing to take risks as traders. Fundamentalists take greater comfort in historical trends and the potential for sustained long-term growth, even to the extent of ignoring and completely discounting the chaos of short-term price movement.

## Key Point

Investors cannot simply become traders overnight. The risk tolerance is different and each discipline defines different kinds of people, with different philosophies about the markets and how to use them.

**failed signal** a technical signal indicating a price direction about to emerge (most notably a price reversal) that does not materialize or is contradicted in actual price movement.

The topic of risk is different from a technical point of view as well. Fundamental risk is related specifically to historical financial strength and operating trends. In comparison, *technical risk* is related to price volatility and trends and to related indicators (like volume, for example) that also are derived from trading action.

Technical risk management requires traders to select stocks for trading that match risk tolerance, and that reflect known volatility the trader finds acceptable. This is very focused, because it involves price as a primary indicator (and for some the only indicator). Compared to fundamental risk management, this is a more concentrated form of risk management. Fundamental analysis has to test many factors including profit and loss, capital strength and working capital, dividend trends, competitive stance within a sector, and quality of management. Technicians seek indicators that anticipate changes in price movement of the stock. There is a lot involved in this process, but the focus is narrow.

An observation of fundamental and technical analysis is often summarized as being the difference between hindsight and foresight, investing and trading, low risk and high risk, or conservative and speculative. These generalizations may apply, but not in every instance. An equally important difference is a reflection of market culture itself. There are significant differences in the perspectives of investors and traders that also show up as different attitudes and opinions between fundamental and technical approaches to the market.

Among the many adages about the market, one applies to help make a distinction between the two groups. That is, "The market rewards patience." Fundamental investors tend to be very patient and methodical in their approach to the market, but technical traders need and want results immediately, perhaps within the trading day.

**chartist**
a trader who studies price patterns through a series of stock charts, looking for early signs for emerging entry or exit points based on how price and volume behave, and using a range of possible technical indicators to make those decisions.

### Key Point

Technical strategists enjoy the excitement and fast action of the market. Fundamental investors are patient and willing to wait for many months, even years, to realize a profit.

Some people on the technical side find the fast entry and exit to be exciting and stimulating, and it is. Traders may be classified as occasional players in the market or as high-volume traders. For example, *day trading* is an activity in which trades tend to be entered and exited within a single trading session. So by the end of the day, no open positions remain.

From a regulatory point of view, day trading presents a problem of a different kind of risk. All margin requirements are based on positions at the end of each trading day, so day traders can execute a high level of trades and use leverage to expose themselves and their brokerage firm to risk, but without incurring any margin requirements. For this reason, a requirement was put in place to identify *pattern day traders* and require them to maintain a minimum cash and securities value of $25,000 in their accounts. This individual is defined as anyone who executes trades in the same stock four times

**technical risk**
any risk directly involving price, reflected in price volatility and trends as well as in related indicators such as trading volume.

**day trading**
activity in which positions are entered and exited on the same day, so that no open positions remain by the end of the day.

**pattern day trader**

any trader who moves in and out of positions in the same stock four or more times within five consecutive trading sessions, who is required to maintain at least $25,000 in cash and securities in their brokerage account.

or more within five consecutive trading sessions. If orders reach this level, they will be banned if the trader does not have an account with the broker with at least $25,000 in cash or securities.

## Valuable Resource

To learn more about the rules governing pattern day traders and margin requirements that apply, go to www.finra.org/Investors/SmartInvesting/ AdvancedInvesting/DayTrading/P005906.

Day traders do not close positions the same day they are opened specifically to get around margin requirements. Many traders believe that trading trends can be identified and acted upon within very short time periods. In fact, one of the amazing facts observed by traders is that chart and price patterns occur regardless of the time duration being studied.

Most people who are not day traders use daily charts as the default time duration, and technical patterns are observed on a day-to-day basis. This works for non–day traders willing to hold positions open for more than a single trading session. The day trader, however, uses charts based on more frequent changes. With the Internet, it is easy to create instant charts and track live feeds for any listed stock, with increments that track on any time period desired. For day traders, five-minute charts provide valuable information about developments in price trends as they evolve.

## Key Point

The observed price patterns that are used to signal entry or exit work in all time durations. So whether you use a daily chart or a five-minute chart, you will find the same technical signals.

The five-minute chart patterns that develop are going to exhibit the same price and chart trends as the daily charts do. However, in a daily chart, the trend encompasses an entire day and many interim price patterns do not show up. So the day trader's argument for more frequent increments in charts is that many entry and exit opportunities are lost in the longer-term chart. Of course, this rapid-action charting system is not for everyone. The dedicated day trader is likely to observe hour-by-hour tendencies in price patterns. A lot of study has gone into analyzing how price trends develop throughout the typical trading day. For example, some traders will tell you not to make trading decisions in the day's first hour. Others believe it is a mistake to put in an order during the Wall Street lunch hour. And many believe that the last hour of the day is when most trends make their move.

| **Key Point** |
| --- |
| Isolating trading activity to specific times of day adds yet another element of timing to the technical decision. Traders find methods that work for them and provide discipline to make their strategies work. |

For anyone inexperienced in trading, the world of day trading is probably too risky. However, the excitement of making decisions by the hour or even by the minute is difficult to match. The more analytical, long-term fundamental approach is comparatively dry and unexciting, even if it may ultimately be more profitable. The truth is that picking high-value stocks and holding them for many months or years is usually profitable, but traders need and want that daily action to make the experience satisfying.

This is the big difference in market culture. The fundamental analyst is likely to be a value investor using a buy-and-hold strategy. The trader, especially the day trader, does not want to own stock for more than the minimum time needed to generate a profit. There are merits and flaws in both systems, without any doubt. It makes the most sense to remain open-minded to both strategies, and even to combine investing and trading in your portfolio.

The next chapter expands on the discussion of trading to examine day trading in more detail, and to compare various trading systems.

**Chapter**

# 7

# Trading Methods: Day and Swing Trading

The basic idea of day trading is not difficult to grasp; but there is more to it than just opening and closing positions on the same day. Day traders employ an array of strategies to improve the timing of their entry and exit. Beyond day trading, an expansion of the concept is called *swing trading*. This is a strategic system involving moving in and out of positions in the short-term, usually three to five days and based on recognition of short-term price trends.

Swing traders rely on specific signals for both entry and exit. These signals warn traders about a trend coming to an end and reversing. This process is an expansion of the same principles used by day traders. This chapter expands on a discussion of these two popular trading systems (day trading and swing trading) and a related topic, entry and exit signals and how to use them.

**swing trading**
a short-term trading strategy based on recognition of trends lasting only a few days (usually three to five), with entry and exit based on set-up signals.

## Day Trading

Day trading is a system involving many technical tools to complete a *round-trip trade* (opening and closing a position) within a single trading session.

**round-trip trade**
the complete steps involved with first opening and then closing a position.

A round-trip trade consists of two major steps: opening and then closing a position. Day traders may be involved in long positions, short positions, or combinations of both. In a long position, the series of steps is buy-hold-sell; with a short position, it is the reverse, or sell-hold-buy.

### Key Point

Day traders prefer closing positions the same day opened, out of concern for potential price differences between today's close and tomorrow's open.

**opening order**
an order placed with a broker to create a position, either long or short.

In all trades, the first step is the *opening order* and the last step is the *closing order*. These are further distinguished by whether either of these is long or short.

An opening order creates either a buy (long) or a sell (short) action. So the distinction *buy to open/sell to open* is critical to ensuring that orders are placed properly. On the closing side, the distinction is just as important. So *sell to close/buy to close* also instructions the broker to enter the order you intend to place.

**closing order**
an order placed with a broker to close a position, whether it was opened long or short.

Day traders have to be familiar with the range of opening and closing orders so that they can avoid placing an order of the wrong type. In addition to mastering order placement terminology, day traders use a series of valuable technical analysis tools, all aimed at helping them to spot trend strength, weakness and reversals, increasing or decreasing momentum, and related volume indicators that help the timing of day trades.

### Key Point

Specific price patterns and changes spark swing trading action, based on short-term trends and reversals.

**buy to open/sell to open**
the type of opening order being placed. A buy to open is used to create a long position, and a sell to open creates a short position.

These technical tools can involve a large number of possible indicators. The most popular and most frequently used are:

1. *Charts.* Indicators most often are spotted visually (even indexed or percentage-based indicators are also charted along with price). Of the many kinds of charts available, candlesticks are becoming very popular with traders (see Chapter 8). These charts provide all of the information about price movement in a single formation: opening and closing price, the session's trading range, and the direction of price movement. The shape of candlesticks is also significant and when two or more sticks are analyzed together, specific patterns provide strong clues about reversal (or continuation) most likely to follow.

**sell to close/ buy to close**
the type of closing order being placed. A sell to close is used to close an existing long position, and a buy to close is used to close an existing short position.

2. *Moving average (MA) analysis.* The moving average is among the most important of technical tools, and day traders more than most technical analysts rely on MA to spot strength or weakness in the current trend. Among the MA analysis is the use of two MA lines of different duration. For example, watching the movement in a 20-day and a 200-day MA is revealing. The *convergence/divergence* of the MA lines tells the technician when price is likely to reverse directions. A popular variation of this is called *MACD*, which is an acronym for moving average convergence/divergence.

**convergence/ divergence**
in technical analysis, the pattern revealed in two moving averages of different numbers of sessions. As the lines move closer together (converge) or farther apart (diverge) the chartist draws conclusions about the coming price direction.

3. *Breadth of trading range analysis.* The trading range is the key to most forms of technical analysis. As this breadth changes, it holds great significance. A broadening breadth reveals growing price volatility; a narrowing breadth tells you two things. First, volatility is declining; second, a reversal from the current trend is quite likely. Chapter 9 includes an explanation of this indicator.

4. *Support- and resistance-based analysis.* Also in chapter 9 is an explanation of a range of popular and valuable technical indicators. The importance of support and resistance is central to all types of technical indicators, and for day traders, these bottom and top trading levels help define risk and potential profits or losses in a short-term strategy.

**MACD**
a popular technical indicator, meaning moving average convergence/ divergence, the study of trends based on the proximity between price and averages.

Day traders use a specific type of strategic timing approach to the market. However, even traders who hold positions open beyond a single trading session most often use the same strategies, but across a less frantic pace. Day traders are specifically associated with some focused trading activities.

### Key Point

Variations in day trading include very specific recognition tools; variations in day trading extend beyond single-session open and close activity.

The first style is called *intra-day trading*. A day trader normally opens and closes a position in a single day. The intra-day trader might do the same, or leave a position open until the following session. The usual pattern is for the position to remain open for a period of time between a few minutes and two trading sessions.

**intra-day trading**
a variation of day trading, a strategy in which positions are opened and closed within single trading sessions or, at the most, two consecutive sessions.

Day traders rely on a series of specific entry and exit signals, which are explained later in this chapter. A variation of this approach is *momentum trading*. Under this system, trades are opened and then closed based on a short-term trend (this may last only a matter of minutes, or for entire trading day). The ideal momentum trade is made at the beginning of the trend and then closed as soon as momentum becomes exhausted or reverses.

Why is momentum trading any different from other approaches to day trading? Momentum traders act specifically on perceived direction of price, and on slowing down of the pace as a reversal and exit signal. A momentum trader is also likely to analyze price trends using extremely short trading increments, such as five-minute charts. In comparison, other day traders are likely to study price patterns and tests of support and resistance to find entry and exit points, and may use charts taking more time, such as one-hour charts, for example. The momentum trader only tracks the direction of price, and other day traders are likely to seek patterns anticipating reversal before it actually occurs.

### Key Point

Day and swing traders look for specific price-related patterns. Momentum traders focus on price direction and strength of timing movement.

Another advanced system, one used by momentum traders and other day traders, is to analyze the price action within a single day using multiple time increments. For example, you might combine analysis using 5-minute, 15-minute, and 60-minute charts. This achieves multiple views of the same price, based on the fact that some developing reversal points may be hidden in the longer-duration charts but show up in the 5- or 15-minute versions of the same stock. Chartists who watch two or three different charts at the same time understand that price patterns form in all time increments, and they want to be sure they have all of the visual tools possible. A trader using this strategy is also likely to move in and out of positions more frequently than other day traders, based mostly on changes in momentum.

**momentum trading**
a system of day trading based solely on identifying short-term trends and timing entry and exit based on the trend's strength or weakness (momentum).

The desire to close positions before the end of the trading day is characteristic of day traders. The criticism that this avoids the legal margin requirements is part of the reason, but not the primary reason that day traders want to move in and out before trading stops. Most day traders do not want to leave their positions open overnight based on the fear that big changes can occur from one session to the next.

In a nicely ordered world, a stock would open close to the price it closed the day before. However, with growing interest in after-hours trading, this is not a certainty. Companies also tend to make earnings and other announcements after the close of trading just to avoid a big impact on the stock's price on the day the announcement is made. So day traders have a point in wanting to be out of open positions; there are just too many variables that can develop. The chance of a big price change between today's close and tomorrow's open is a very real possibility.

---

### Key Point

Yesterday's close and tomorrow's open are not always the same, and often are not even close. This provides a clue about why day traders are concerned about leaving positions open overnight.

---

Unlike the buy-and-hold investor who thinks in terms of years, traders think in terms of minutes or hours and act accordingly. Over recent years, the average holding period of positions—including both investors and traders—has been on the decline. Figure 7.1 demonstrates the history of average holding periods since 1920.

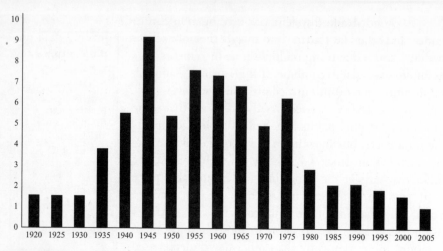

**FIGURE 7.1** Average holding period, stocks.
*Source*: New York Stock Exchange (NYSE) data.

The trend demonstrated that between 1945 and 1980, the buy-and-hold philosophy reigned within the stock market, and then declined rapidly. Today, trading has replaced a lot of the traditional strategies that value investing supports—even in spite of the successful track record of the buy-and-hold approach.

The causes of these changes, notably after 1975, are varied. Before 1975, average holding period was higher than four years each and every year. From 1980 onward, the average fell below three years and remained there. In 2005, for the first time, the average holding period was less than one year. The Internet has made trading easier than ever before, explaining a part of the trend since 2000; but the trend predates the Internet, so a broader trend has been underway. It might be related to the timing of major market primary trends. For example, after the 1929 crash, average holding period rose until 1945, after which the decline began.

**Key Point**

A long-term trend in the market is for stock holding periods to decline over time. Most recently, the average has fallen below one year for the first time.

Whatever the cause, the value investing philosophy of buy and hold has lost popularity in recent years and activities like day trading have become increasingly popular. This trend might provide clues to what is going to happen in the future. Investors and traders both play a role in influencing long-term price trends of individual stocks and of the entire market; but no one can say with certainty which group will prevail in future years.

Day traders, like long-term investors, understand the adage that "the trend is your friend." The timeframe, however, is quite different. Buy-and-hold proponents may criticize the extremely short-term mindset of the day trader by expanding the adage to "the trend is your friend—until the end." In other words, an accumulation of small, rapid profits can be wiped out in one ill-timed move.

# Swing Trading

Day trading and intra-day trading focus intentionally on very short entry-to-exit timeframes. Traders use charts of very small time spans, and may take profits within a matter of moments. In comparison, swing trading uses many of the same short-term trend and reversal signals, but involves a holding period of at least three days, and in most applications, not more than five days.

Swing traders rely on specific *set-up signals* for both entry and exit. Because swing traders are playing the swing of price, the current trend's exit set-up may also serve as the next swing's entry set-up.

There are four important price patterns for swing trading. These are:

1. *Three or more short-term trending days.* A "trend" is very specific manner under the rules of swing trading. An *uptrend* is a series of consecutive sessions characterized by each session showing a higher high price than the previous session, and also showing a higher low price. These higher highs and higher lows must occur at least over three sessions.

   For example, a three-day series consists of high–low prices of $24–22, $27–23, and $28–25. This is an uptrend because over the three sessions both the high and low levels increased.

   A *downtrend* is recognized as a series of three or more consecutive sessions characterized by lower highs and lower lows.

   For example, a three-day series consists of high–low prices of $24–22, $23–20, and $21–19. This is a downtrend because over the three sessions both the high and low levels decreased.

2. *An NRD.* The *narrow range day (NRD)* is one with a trading range with opening and closing prices close to one another. The NRD may be relative to preceding sessions; but the closer the opening and

**set-up signals**
patterns or changes in price or volume that tell day traders and swing traders when likely trend reversals are about to take place.

**uptrend**
in swing trading, a series of consecutive sessions with higher high prices and higher low prices in each session, compared to the previous session.

**downtrend**

in swing trading, a series of consecutive sessions with lower high prices and lower low prices in each session, compared to the previous session.

**narrow range day (NRD)**

a trading session in which opening and closing prices are very close or identical, indicating exhausting of the trend and a likely reversal about to occur.

**volume spike**

a single trading session with higher-than-average volume, signaling the possibility of a coming reversal of price movement.

closing prices, the stronger the indication is that a reversal is coming. It indicates that at the end of the trend, the current price is close to agreement between buyers and sellers, or that the trending action has been exhausted.

3. *Exceptionally high volume.* When a *volume spike* occurs, it also signals high chances for a price reversal. The spike occurs for a good reason and may signal that the direction of the existing trend has come to an end, with the other side (buyers versus sellers, or sellers versus buyers) about to take control.

4. *A change in price direction, ending the trend.* When a *reversal day* appears, it clearly ends the trend as defined by swing traders. So a series of upward-moving days concludes with a downward-moving day, or vice versa. This, especially when combined with other reversal signals, is a sign of a broader reversal.

When two or more of these signals occur together, they confirm one another and provide the strongest possible indication that the price is likely to stop moving in the established direction and will probably turn and move in the opposite direction.

---

**Key Point**

As valuable as reversal signals are that swing traders use, when two or more show up together, the strength of the confirmation is very strong.

---

The philosophy behind swing trading is based on two observations. First is the basic contrarian strategy. This is the belief that the majority is more often wrong than right. So when prices begin moving upward, a growing number of people buy, with most buyers at the top of the short-term trend. And when prices begin moving downward, a growing number of people sell, with most sellers at the bottom of the short-term trend.

Second is the belief that market decisions are made based on two primary emotions: greed and fear. As prices rise, new buyers come in to get a piece of the action and existing owners of stock do not take profits, because they do not want to miss out on even higher gains. When prices fall, current owners of stock panic and sell, mostly at the bottom of the price swing.

The swing traders acknowledge the strength of greed and fear as motivating forces in the market, but they resist acting in response. They make decisions rationally and without emotion. When greed drives prices up, swing traders look for the signs that the trend is slowing or coming to an end. When that happens, they sell long positions or open short positions. When prices are falling, swing traders wait for signals that the trend is bottoming out. At that point, they buy to close any short positions, or open long positions.

> **reversal day**
> the end of a trend; a session that moves in the direction opposite the established direction, signaling a high possibility of a reversal in the price direction.

This swing is normally going to last between three and five sessions. Swing traders want to move in and out of positions that quickly, because part of the strategy recognizes that the short-term emotional reaction is always exaggerated; but it also corrects at the end of that three- to five-day period. In fact, it is the emotional reaction and overreaction that creates the short-term swing.

## Entry and Exit Signals

The dilemma most traders are aware of is *when* to enter a position. But there is more. After you enter, you also need to know when and why to exit the position. Both of these decisions can be based on gut reaction (greed and fear dominating), or on a logical assessment of the price for the stock and recognition of the nonemotional reasons for moving.

Just as investors need to set goals for exiting positions based on profit targets or loss bail-out points, traders also need to know when to sell. When you are operating based on one of the several theories of trading, you really are not aware of risk. That awareness only takes hold once real money is placed into a trade. This is why setting very clear entry and exit rules for yourself is essential to trading success.

> **Key Point**
>
> Even if you understand the steps and techniques of trading, you do not truly appreciate risk until you have actual money committed to a position.

**congestion**
a price pattern
of sideways
movement
within a narrow
trading range,
with neither
buyers nor
sellers in
control.

One of the confusing patterns you see time and again is a *congestion* pattern in price. This occurs after a trend has ended and before another trend begins. Congestion can last two or three sessions or for an entire month or more. Prices move sideways without making any clear moves in either direction. Another name for this could be "confusion" because neither buyers nor sellers are in control, and no one can decide which way prices are going to move next.

During periods of congestion, patterns are going to emerge, giving you a clue about trends about to emerge.

It often occurs that traders wait out the congestion hoping to spot a strong trend; but by the time the trend is apparent, the opportunity has been lost. This is a dangerous point in the trend. Some movement away from congestion could end up as a failed signal. The danger of making decisions to either enter or exit positions during periods of congestion is in the difficulty of reading when the period is really ending. The solution is to seek out strong signals of a trend, and to not make a move without equally strong confirmation.

It is better to lose an opportunity because of the dangers in trying to read the congestion pattern than to make a decision and end up losing on the trade. If you consider the patterns taking place right before congestion, the confusion makes sense. It is likely to follow a period of very strong trending price action, even including strong or consecutive price gaps and then exhaustion. At this point, when momentum has been used up, neither buyers nor sellers are able to create movement. This is when failed signals may develop. It isn't so much that the signal is deceptive, but that it lacks the strength to continue in the direction indicated.

### Key Point

In periods of congestion, the uncertainty confuses the decision-making process even with signals; you are better off missing an opportunity than risking a loss in these conditions.

Confirmation may come in the form of two or more reversal or entry signals (initiation of a trend of three or more days, an NRD, or a volume spike). Remember, when two or more of these show up together, it is an exceptionally strong indication that prices are about to begin trending. However, today charts are available to everyone with a computer and knowledge about technical analysis is more widespread than ever. This does not necessarily mean that indicators are interpreted accurately; in fact, with the widespread access there is a tendency to oversimplify the meaning of indicators. Trading is not a formula that works every time; you cannot see a signal and act on it with certainty. Rather, the accurate interpretation of technical indicators should improve the frequency of being right, improving your averages rather than creating sure-fire systems for profitability.

Exit profits can be summarized as percentage gain/loss or dollar amounts. These should be realistic and moderate and, most important, once you set your exit standards, you have to follow your own rules. Otherwise, the exercise contains no value.

Traders make some recurring errors that can be avoided as long as you know about them. These are:

- Trying to make profits on a trade adequate to make up for a loss previously experienced (this increases your risk exposure and usually will not work out profitably).
- Converting small losses into large losses.
- Dwelling on a loss or poorly timed trade rather than learning from it and moving on.
- Setting unrealistic goals, notably excessively high profits, which ensures you will rarely meet those goals.

### Key Point

Traders are at risk of making errors in their approach to trades; the solution is to set clear policies and then follow your own rules.

For entry and exit, note the following signals that provide you with the strongest and best action points:

- In *all* cases, even a strong indicator should be confirmed. This may be a matter of confirming an NRD with a reversal day or volume spike, or seeing a three-session trend coming out of confirmation, along with an NRD.
- Look for gapping action or, as they say in London's Underground subway system, "Mind the Gap." Gaps are very significant because they imply that buyers (upside gaps) or sellers (downside gaps) are making their move. Gaps are especially meaningful when they occur as part of a breakout above resistance or below support. However, before jumping in, look for confirmation of a new trend; the gap may reverse and fill, retreating to the established trading range, making it a failed signal.

- Breakouts that hold and continue to move represent a strong signal, assuming confirmation occurs as well by way of gaps, three or more trending sessions, or other strong indicators.

- You are going to create more profits by getting in at the proper moment, which is right after confirmation but before the crowd acts. If you wait, it will be too late. Traders who lead rather than follow are going to have more profits.

- The traditional technical signs, like tests of resistance or support, head and shoulders, and triangles, are valuable confirming patterns but are but not as reliable on their own as the swing trade reversal signs (NRDs, volume spikes, and reversal days after short-term trends).

**percentage swing**

price movement of a specified percentage below the high or above the low, used to generate entry or exit decisions as part of a swing trading strategy.

To accurately decide when to enter or exit, you may select from a number of signals and confirmation. However, the ideal indicator is not always going to show up, so an alternative is to look for a percentage of price movement above or below a previous level and use this as the decision point. You decide to buy if the price movement is downward a specific percentage from the high; you sell if the price movement is upward from the low. This *percentage swing* approach provides you with a framework and discipline that programs your decision point; it is based on the observed tendency for price to go through predictable swings in three to five days.

### Key Point

Using the percentage swing method gives you clear signals for timing entry and exit; this helps overcome confusion and uncertainty, even in volatile markets.

The desirability of percentage swing is that entry and exit are automatic, assuming you follow the rules you establish within the swing. The percentage that you select depends on your risk tolerance as a trader, and on different degrees of change for entry and for exit. For example, if you are out of a swing trade and you use percentage swing to reenter, you may set the percentage at 5 percent or 10 percent. If too high, you may never reach the point; if too low, you might enter too soon. For exit, you might have a greater sensitivity to loss, meaning a loss percentage might be lower than a gain percentage.

Percentage swing is a good system, at least to generate your attention. However, it works best as a first step in the decision, which should not be made until a confirming signal develops. It is possible that a percentage will occur, but the other signals have not developed or you even see a contradictory signal (in technical indicators, candlestick formations, or other methods you employ). In those situations, use percentage swing as one among many different signal points you employ as part of your timing strategies.

### Key Point

Percentage swing is best used as a generating change, but the movement should be confirmed by other indicators before you act.

In calculating the percentage swing, it is not always necessary to restrict the test to the change within a single trading session. In periods of great volatility between sessions, you may calculate and track a stock's *true range* between the previous day's closing price and the current day's high price. This encompasses a range well beyond a single session's opening and closing, and may provide more significant insights in the price movement and the timing of your entry or exit.

**true range**
a recalculated trading range including not only a single session, but the range between one session's closing price and the next session's high.

True range analysis may absorb the day-to-day *gapping behavior* that otherwise clouds judgment and makes interpretation difficult. Not all gaps are visible, either, so true range analysis helps to clarify the situation especially when price volatility is high. These day-to-day gaps are not always visible. For example, if yesterday's price opened at $26 and closed at $23, and today's price opened at $20 and closed at $24, there was a three-point gap between the two sessions. However, on a candlestick chart the two sessions overlap, so the gap is not as visible as one in which both sessions move in the same direction.

**gapping behavior**
differences in price levels between one day's closing price and the next day's opening price, especially when this incidence is repetitive or frequent.

It also helps to see gaps if you combine daily sessions with higher-volume interim charts. For example, you might see frequent gaps on a one-hour chart that do not show up at all in the full-day chart. This does not mean the day's session is any more volatile than average; it does provide you with insight about trading action during the session rather than the summarized range information for the entire day. In the true range version of a trading range, the high price is either today's high or yesterday's close, and the low is either today's low or yesterday's close. This system applies in looking backward on daily charts, or in performing the same function on one-hour or even more frequent charts during the day.

---

### Key Point

Gapping behavior may be invisible, not only between sessions but even within a single session; combining daily charts with higher-frequency charts like one-hour or 20-minute charts helps spot volatility within the session.

---

Regardless of the duration of your sessions, it is important to understand that gapping behavior affects the conclusions you draw. For example, in a percentage swing, do you use today's opening price as your point of comparison? Or do you use yesterday's closing price? If these have gapped overnight, the analysis could be rendered inaccurate if you limit it to the current session only.

The real key to ensuring your analysis of price movement is accurate interpretation of charts. The next chapter explores charting and the many tools you can find in single-session or multiple-session trends.

**Chapter**

# Charting Tools and Interpretation

T raders rely on charts. They study and analyze charts not only to spot price trends, but also to decide when to enter or exit a position. This is the key to trading. It is not enough to identify a stock that you like, or that you believe is going to move in the direction you desire. You also need to determine precisely when to enter a position and when to exit.

This is no small matter. It takes considerable study and analysis to develop a sense of the many timing signals that you need and will use to improve the timing of trades. These set-up signals can include a short-term trend as it begins or ends, volume levels, traditional technical signs like gaps and breakouts from the established trading range, and specific price patterns you find on charts.

**Key Point**

Entry and exit timing signals are numerous and not always easy to spot. It requires experience and practice to fine-tune the skill traders rely upon to time their trading decisions.

Technical indicators are keys to improving your chart-based analysis. The premise of this range of tools rests with the trading range and well-defined levels of support and resistance. More specifically, conclusions are reached by how price acts and tests these trading range borders. The technical indicators based on the theory of trading range patterns are collectively called *Western technical indicators* and are based on interpretations traditionally performed through the development of charts over a period of days, weeks, and months. They focus on price and volume changes and developing levels of momentum. This chapter is focused specifically on various kinds of charts that you will use to study price patterns and improve your timing.

Before the widespread use of the Internet and easy access to free and instantaneous online charting, traders had to build their own charts by plotting prices each day and hoping to identify opportunities to enter positions or changing trends to generate well-timed exits. By today's standards, these old-style methods are quite primitive. Today, traders are more likely to use *Eastern technical indicators*. This is a method of analysis and timing based on the study of *candlestick* charting.

This chapter explains various types of charts and then focuses on how candlesticks, also called *Japanese candlesticks*, are used effectively not only to improve what charts reveal, but provide extremely valuable patterns in single sessions, double sessions, and triple sessions that reveal likely price direction about to occur.

## Traditional Types of Charts

Candlestick charts would be very difficult to use if you had to construct them by hand for a long series of trading sessions. The Internet has changed all of that, making charts of all kinds easy to tailor and instantly available.

### Key Point

The Internet has made trading fast, efficient, and easy. However, this means that the potential for losses is equally fast, efficient, and easy. The Internet does not ensure profits; it exposes you to greater potential *and* to greater danger.

Before the modern era, traders relied on services to provide charts to them or they had to build them by hand. The most basic kind of chart is the *line chart*, which is simply a line tracking a stock's value over time. The value used is usually the day's ending price.

A typical line chart is shown in Figure 8.1. This is a chart for three months for Home Depot (HD).

This chart provides you with a very simple summary of the sequence of closing prices on each session. As a broad overview of Home Depot's price history, this is useful; but it does not provide any useful intelligence about the trend within the price, or of what is likely to happen next. For this you need to be able to analyze each day's opening and closing price as well as the complete trading range (the range usually includes some movement above and below the opening and closing levels).

**Japanese candlesticks**
alternative name for candlesticks and for the charts on which they are used.

**line chart**
a simplified chart for tracking a stock's price, consisting of a single line connected between days, and normally reflecting the stock's closing price for each session.

---

**Key Point**

The value of charted information is important because you need to see not only the current price, but how that has changed from session to session and within each session.

---

**FIGURE 8.1**  Home Depot (HD), line chart.
Chart courtesy of StockCharts.com.

**OHLC chart**
a stock chart showing each session's trading range by way of a vertical stick, as well as opening and closing price noted by small horizontal sticks.

An example of a chart that was a favorite before candlesticks caught on is the *OHLC chart*. This is an abbreviation of the four main features, "open, high, low, close," that are summarized on the chart.

The same history of Home Depot, but in OHLC format, is shown in Figure 8.2. Although the history is identical, the detail is much greater on the OHLC than on the relatively simple line chart. The vertical stick on each session represents the full trading range for the day. The small horizontal protrusion on the left is the opening price, and the one on the right is the closing price. The distance in between these two is the breadth of the day, or the distance between opening and closing.

When the closing price is higher than the opening price, the session moved upward; when lower, the session moved downward. The nice feature of the OHLC chart is that it is very simple but provides all of the information that you need. The main disadvantage is that spotting trends or significant patterns is quite difficult.

---

### Key Point

The OHLC chart is an efficient but rudimentary way to pick up all of a session's important information, but it is not visually easy to track price or to spot short-term trends.

---

**FIGURE 8.2**  Home Depot (HD), OHLC chart.
Chart courtesy of StockCharts.com.

Both line chart and OHLC provide some level of information, but today the most popular chart is the candlestick chart. This provides all that you need, at a glance, to identify not only the trading range but also the direction of price movement for each session and within a multisession trend.

## Candlestick Charts: The Basics

**real body**
the middle rectangle of a candlestick, showing whether the session moved upward (white) or downward (black), and making it possible to spot trends immediately.

The candlestick is valuable because it conveys a great amount of information in a relatively simple shape: a triangle with a "wick" above, below, or on both ends. The same Home Depot chart in candlestick form is shown in Figure 8.3.

The features of the candlestick include the *real body*, which is the rectangle. If it is white or clear, the session moved upward; is it is black, the session moved downward. The advantage to this feature should be obvious; you can immediately spot trends over a series of sessions when the color of the real body is the same during the period.

The sticks above or below the real body represent the full trading range of the day. The upper and lower horizontal lines of the triangle represent the opening

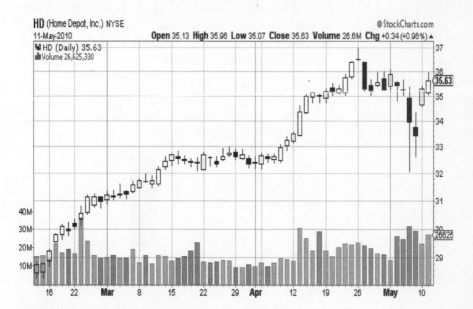

**FIGURE 8.3** Home Depot (HD), candlestick chart.
Chart courtesy of StockCharts.com.

and closing prices; the body itself is the distance between opening and closing. The sticks above and below the real body are the complete trading range for the day. These are called the *shadows* and are also called *tails* when exceptionally long, or *wicks*. The "tail" form of a shadow often has extra significance because it represents a failed attempt to move price farther than the opening/closing range.

The shadows are given additional names that tell you whether price moved above or below the real body. The *upper shadow* represents price action that was bullish, or an attempt to move prices higher even though the day's prices closed below that level. The *lower shadow* is the range of prices below the real body, or an attempt to move prices lower that failed, and with prices returning to the real body before the end of the session.

The complete candlestick shows you not only direction for the sessions, but for a range of sessions. The different segments of the candlestick are shown in Figure 8.4.

Referring back to the Home Depot candlestick chart in Figure 8.3, how much can you discover from this chart? This period began with a nice uptrend including some gapping patterns. It ended with a middle period of sideways movement, or congestion, in which neither buyers nor sellers had control. This lasted nearly a full month, from the middle of March until the middle of April. The uptrend then resumed.

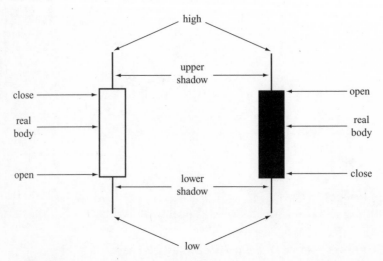

**FIGURE 8.4**   Candlestick segments.

### Key Point

A comparison between the same data on an OHLC chart and a candlestick chart demonstrates the vast difference and shows that candlesticks are easier to use and interpret.

**upper shadow**
the vertical portion of a candlestick extending above the real body and representing a failed attempt during the session to move the price higher.

Notice the fourth day of the uptrend. It was accompanied by very high volume, confirming the resumption of a bullish trend. Another very clear signal occurred at the very top of the uptrend. The narrow range day (NRD) at the very top is given the name *doji* in candlestick analysis. The word *doji* means "mistake" and it is easy to spot. The distance between opening and closing prices is very small or those levels are identical. So instead of a rectangle, a doji session is a horizontal line.

In the case of Home Depot (Figure 8.3), the doji at the very top of the uptrend was a clear reversal signal. Note the upper shadow, which was an attempt to move price further upward. Its failure signals a loss of momentum and a high likelihood of a reversal and price decline.

While there are dozens of candlestick formations that provide excellent insight into price movement, momentum, continuation, and reversal, following are some of the major ones worth paying attention to. These recur often at key points in a price trend and can be valuable to signal reversal and to confirm what other indicators also reveal.

**lower shadow**
the vertical portion of a candlestick extending below the real body and representing a failed attempt during the session to move the price lower.

**doji**
a candlestick with little or no distance between opening and closing, so that a horizontal line is found instead of a rectangle.

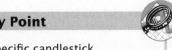

### Key Point

There are so many specific candlestick formations that they are rich analytical tools; at the same time it takes practice and study to master the range of indicators in the form of candlestick sessions.

The first group worth analyzing is the single-stick candle. This is a candlestick of a single day that holds special meaning and also provides valuable

**long candle**
a candle with
an unusually
long real body,
either white or
black, and likely
to foreshadow
reversal when it
appears at the
end of a trend.

**continuation day**
a single day with
a candlestick
pattern
providing a sign
of a continuation
in the trend
rather than
reversal, due to
its position and
direction within
the trend.

**marubozu**
a long candle,
white or black,
with either no
shadows or only
a shadow above
or below the real
body.

insight about the current trend. Single-stick formations include the following:

*Long candles.* A long candle is any candlestick, white or black, with an exceptionally wide breadth between opening and closing price. A long white candle appearing at or near the bottom of a downtrend is a strong reversal signal; it shows that buyers controlled price action throughout the day. A long black candle showing up at the top of an uptrend has the same meaning, a likely reversal and start of a downtrend.

The long candle may also appear in the middle of a trend. If the color of the candle is consistent with the trend direction (white in uptrends or black in downtrends), it may serve as a *continuation day* or indicator.

A variation of the long candle is the *marubozu*. In Japanese, this word means "little hair." It is called this because it is a long candle with one of three features: it either has no shadows, or only an upper shadow, or only a lower shadow.

The marubozu with neither shadow is the strongest sign of a bullish trend (white marubozu) or a bearish trend (black marubozu).

The long candlestick types are summarized in Figure 8.5.

*Short candles.* On the opposite side of the scale of single-day candles is the short candle. The extreme version of this is the previously mentioned doji, which comes in several varieties. Every doji consists of a horizontal line instead of a rectangular real body; the opening and closing price for the session is identical or extremely close together. A *dragonfly doji* has a lower shadow, so it forms a capital letter T. The extent of the lower shadow determines the strength; the lower the shadow, the stronger. If a dragonfly doji shows up at the bottom of the trend, it is extremely bullish because the attempted move downward failed.

The opposite of the dragonfly is the *gravestone doji*, which has only an upper shadow and looks like a capital T turned upside down. When this appears at the top of an uptrend, it is a very strong reversal indicator.

The short candlestick types are summarized in Figure 8.6.

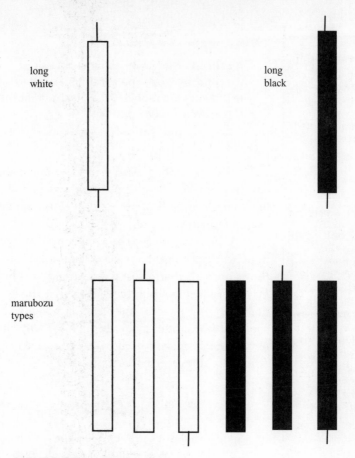

**FIGURE 8.5** Long candles.

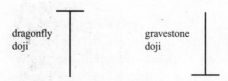

**FIGURE 8.6** Short candles.

*Trend-based candles.* Some single-stick candles have a meaning that relies on the current market conditions. These are bullish, bearish, and sideways. So a specific candlestick might appear but its interpretation relies on these conditions.

**dragonfly doji**
a bullish doji with a lower shadow only, recognizable by its formation of a capital letter T.

**gravestone doji**
a bearish doji
with an upper
shadow only,
which looks like
a capital T turned
upside down.

## Key Point

A general observation about candlesticks:
exceptionally long and exceptionally short
real bodies are probably the most significant
signals you are going to see.

The first among these is the *long-legged doji*, which
has exceptionally long upper *and* lower shadows. The
horizontal real body appears closer to the middle of the
overall formation.

A long-legged doji showing up at the top of an
uptrend signals possible reversal and is bearish; when it
shows up at the bottom of a downtrend, it is bullish and
may signal a coming uptrend. However, the long-legged
doji (like any pattern) may also fail and in hindsight
could be a misleading indicator. This is why all patterns
in candlestick analysis need to be confirmed before entry
or exit decisions are finalized.

**long-legged doji**
a doji with
exceptionally
long upper and
lower shadows,
with the small
real body about
halfway in the
formation. This
may be bullish
or bearish
depending
on where it
appears in the
trend.

## Key Point

Some candlestick sessions, like the long-legged
doji, may be either bullish or bearish depending
on where they show up.

Another candle that depends on where it shows
up is the *spinning top*. This is a candle with a small real
body of either color, and long upper and lower shadows. It is similar to the long-legged doji, and like the
doji, the spinning top's real body should appear about
halfway through the formation.

A spinning top is a buy signal when it shows up
at the bottom of a downtrend, or a sell signal at the top
of an uptrend. Reversal works in both conditions and
the important feature is placement along with shape; the
color of the real body is incidental.

**spinning top**
a candle with
a small real
body and long
upper and
lower shadows
of about the
same size; the
spinning top is
either bullish
or bearish,
depending
on where it is
found.

> ## · Key Point
>
> A spinning top candlestick, like the long-legged doji, may be bullish or bearish. It depends on where it appears.

A final single-stick development that appears a lot is the *hammer* or *hanging man*. These both consist of a small real body (color does not matter) and a long lower shadow with no upper shadow. When this shows up at the bottom of a downtrend, it is a bullish reversal signal and is called a hammer. If it shows up at the top of an uptrend, it is a bearish reversal and is called a hanging man.

The trend-based candlestick types are summarized in Figure 8.7.

*Two-stick patterns.* Another group of candlesticks worth noting involves two consecutive sessions. The *engulfing pattern* consists of a set-up day that has a smaller rectangle on both sides, with the second day's real body extending beyond. The second day's high is higher, and its low is lower than the day preceding. The bullish version consists of a black set-up session and a white second session; the bearish version is the opposite, with a white set-up and black second session.

**hammer**
a candle with a small real body of either color, and a long lower shadow. It appears at the bottom of a downtrend and, if confirmed, indicates a bullish reversal.

Another two-stick pattern is called a *harami*. In Japanese, this word means "pregnant." This is the opposite of the engulfing pattern and consists of a set-up day that has a higher high and a higher low than the second day. A bullish version has a black set-up and a white second day; and a bearish version has a white set-up day and a black second day.

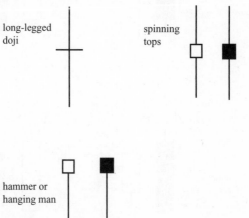

**FIGURE 8.7** Trend-based candles.

Dozens of additional two-stick patterns also can be used for reversal signals, confirmation, and continuation indicators. The preceding are only the most prominent and widely used among them.

**hanging man**
a candle with a small real body of either color, and a long lower shadow. It appears at the top of an uptrend and, if confirmed, indicates a bearish reversal.

### Key Point

There are dozens of two-stick candlestick indicators. Some are more subtle than others; they provide excellent forms of initial indicators or confirmation signals.

The two-stick candlestick types are summarized in Figure 8.8.

*Three-stick patterns.* The most complex but also the strongest of candlestick indicators are made up of three consecutive sessions. There are dozens of these and, like the single- and double-stick patterns, the following are only the most easily found and most common of the three-stick patterns.

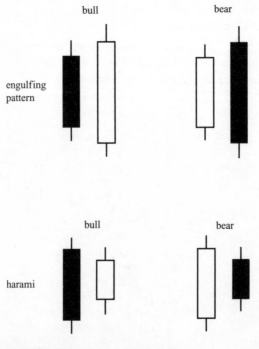

**FIGURE 8.8** Two-stick candles.

**Key Point**

Three-stick indicators are the strongest of all. Because there are three consecutive sessions in each pattern, they serve as a mini-trend of their own.

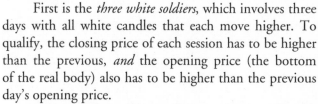

**Key Point**

Three-stick indicators are the strongest of all. Because there are three consecutive sessions in each pattern, they serve as a mini-trend of their own.

**engulfing pattern**
a two-session candlestick formation with the second day longer on both sides of the first day (engulfing its range). A bullish version consists of a black set-up day and a white second day; a bearish version consists of a white set-up and a black second day.

First is the *three white soldiers*, which involves three days with all white candles that each move higher. To qualify, the closing price of each session has to be higher than the previous, *and* the opening price (the bottom of the real body) also has to be higher than the previous day's opening price.

The opposite of the bullish three white soldiers is the bearish *three black crows* pattern. This is a series of black candles. Each day's opening price is lower than the previous day's open, and each closing is lower than the previous day's close.

Another interesting three-day pattern is the *squeeze alert*. A bullish version looks like the three black crows with an important difference. All three sessions are black, but each day's range is lower on both sides. Each reports a lower high and a higher low. The bearish squeeze alert is the opposite and it is similar to the three white soldiers. However, each session's high is lower than the previous; and each session's low is higher than the previous.

The three-stick candlestick types are summarized in Figure 8.9.

Many additional candlesticks are found in the study of charts, and work well to confirm indicated reversal and continuation patterns. The preceding is only an introductory look at candlesticks. The range of possible signals is vast, with more than 100 potential different signals consisting of single sticks or two-day or three-day formations.

**harami**
a two-candlestick pattern with a set-up day containing a higher high and a lower low. A bull harami consists of a black set-up followed by a white day; and a bear harami has a white set-up day followed by a black second day.

**Key Point**

Candlestick analysis is not a technique you will pick up quickly. The more you study it, the more you discover that a wide range of patterns identifies reversal, momentum, and continuation.

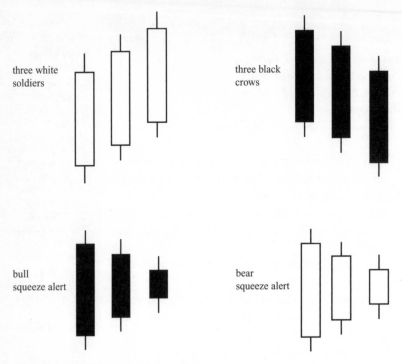

**FIGURE 8.9** Three-stick candles.

## Combining Candlesticks with Western Technical Analysis

**three white soldiers**
a bullish candlestick formation of three consecutive sessions. All three are white. Each day's closing price is higher than the preceding close and each day's opening price is higher than the previous day's open.

The concept of confirmation has been introduced and explained in previous chapters. However, it is more than the verification of what appears to be taking place by seeing the same thing through a second indicator. Confirmation, especially for the timing of entry and exit, involves much more.

Candlesticks—including one-, two-, and three-session patterns—are reliable initial indicators for change in price patterns, especially reversal. So, for example, a day trader or swing trader can use candlesticks to improve timing. Relying on reversal days, NRDs, and volume spikes can be effective as a timing management tool, but when these are combined with candlestick analysis, the technique is far more powerful.

## Key Point

Candlesticks are not stand-alone indicators, but part of a wider system of confirmation between candlesticks and other technical methods.

**three black crows**
a bearish candlestick formation of three consecutive sessions. All three are black. Each day's closing price is lower than the preceding close and each day's opening price is lower than the previous day's open.

In that sense, confirmation does include two or more independent indicators pointing in the same direction; but it also is made more effective by being put into action as a cross-disciplinary tool. So candlesticks, which are Eastern, are effectively employed with the traditional Western signals that chartists and day or swing traders rely upon. This can work in either direction. An initial indicator may be Eastern or Western and then be confirmed by the other side.

This makes candlestick charting very effective as part of a broader timing strategy. In addition to verification by way of two or more signals, the independent sources and theories of how those signals develop strengthen the confirmation.

The key to Western technical theories is the basic support and resistance that define the current trading range, and the way that price patterns approach these borders, break through them, continue or retreat, and create or lose momentum. The next chapter summarizes the essential tools of technical analysis; remember, however, that these are going to be most effective when used along with candlestick chart patterns as forms of confirmation.

**squeeze alert**
a series of three consecutive candle sessions. A bull squeeze alert consists of black candles, and a bear squeeze alert has three white candles. In both cases, each day's high is lower than the previous; and each day's low is higher than the previous.

**Chapter**

# Essential Technical Indicators

The topic of technical analysis has filled many books that still only scratched the surface. This chapter is by no means an exhaustive explanation of the entire realm of technical analysis; however, it does provide a summary of the most important concepts and indicators that technical analysts rely upon to analyze price movement.

The difference between fundamental and technical is a good starting point for understanding how it all works. Both disciplines are most effective when used together because each side approaches analysis from a different perspective. The collective insights you gain by combining the fundamental and the technical are more valuable than either analytical school of thought can provide alone.

---

### Key Point

Fundamental and technical analyses begin from different starting points, making them most valuable when used together.

---

Technical analysis relies on the study of price patterns and trends of stocks. Fundamental analysis relies on the study of historical financial results and capitalization of companies. Both are intended to help select companies and their stocks, even though they come to the question with vastly different assumptions. Because fundamental science is historical and focused on the company, it is the favored technique for investors. This contrasts with traders, who focus on timing of entry and exit in positions in the short term, with little focus on long-term investment value or comparative quality of the company itself.

It is not only possible, but wise, for an individual to devote a share of the overall portfolio to each side. Thus, you build a long-term portfolio of stocks based on the principles of value investing, and you also use a portion of capital for short-term trading based on current market conditions and the rise and fall of prices. In order to accomplish this two-part strategic method, you need to understand the basics of both sides. Following are the highlights of basic technical analysis every trader needs to master.

## Support and Resistance: The Trading Range as a Defining Attribute of Price

Most traders have heard about support and resistance; but few truly understand how significant it is and how it serves as the basis for virtually every technical indicator.

When you go through a list of technical signs and signals, you discover that most of them are given importance based on how they interact with support and resistance. These defining borders of the trading range provide a sense of order and predictability to analysis. When price levels remain within the trading range, it leads to a specific conclusion; when price breaks out above resistance or below support, it leads to a completely different conclusion.

| **Key Point** |
| --- |
| Practically all technical indicators are based on a comparison between price action and support and resistance. |

A price breakout may retreat to the previously established trading range. If that occurs, it is likely to take place fairly quickly after the breakout. If price continues to move above or below the previous range, it probably means a new trading range is being set.

When price moves out of the current trading range, how do you decide where the new borders should be set? For some traders, the violation of a trading range leads to a period of chaos and uncertainty. Until a new, clearly defined border is set, they cannot rely on price trends. However, an interesting phenomenon occurs in some instances, in which the previous level of resistance becomes the new level of support, or the previous support becomes the new resistance.

This *range flip* can be used to set a new test for subsequent price movement. If the newly observed resistance or support is later violated in a price reversal, it means the new level of trading will not hold. If the new level is tested but prices remain within its border, it means the newly set range is permanent.

For example, the chart for Altria (MO) in Figure 9.1 demonstrates how this flip takes place and how it appears.

In this example, prices moved above the resistance level and remained there. The previous resistance became support and was tested, seen at the point where two consecutive sessions exhibited long lower shadows but closed above the new support level. This indicates that the new support was strong; because it held at the test, a trader should have confidence in this new support.

**range flip**
the observed change after a price breakout, in which previous resistance becomes new support in an uptrend, or in which previous support becomes new resistance in a downtrend.

## Key Point

The tendency for support and resistance to flip after a successful price breakout is an important clue for traders; this helps add confidence in new trading levels, or to test whether the breakout is going to succeed or fail.

**FIGURE 9.1** Range flip, example 1.
Chart courtesy of StockCharts.com.

Another example is found in the three-month chart of the same period for Wal-Mart (WMT), as shown in Figure 9.2. This is an example of previous support flipping over to new resistance.

In this situation, the established trading range was newly established but, as the chart reveals, did not last for long. The support level flipped over to become new resistance. This was tested to a degree but it held. In this situation, it appeared that the brief upward movement did not last, and that there was a retreat down to the previous range. The new resistance level (previously the support level) was accompanied by a new support level very close to the original support shown three months earlier.

Support and resistance bring order to what would otherwise look like a completely chaotic price trend. The Wal-Mart three-month chart appears at first glance to be moving all over the map, but when you analyze the exchange between support and resistance, notably with (a) the flip and (b) the reversion to a previous level of support, it becomes clear that there is considerable order in the long-term trend.

The established trading levels define volatility, another name for market risk. The wider the trading range breadth, the greater the volatility; *and* the more often a breakout occurs (even if prices eventually retreat), the less certainty a trader can have in the price trend. This is especially true if the price history

**FIGURE 9.2** Range flip, example 2.
Chart courtesy of StockCharts.com.

includes many gaps. The bigger the gaps, the more volatile the price and the less predictable the future.

The trading borders are so crucial to most types of technical analysis because price levels take on meaning when these borders are tested. When you review any form of price pattern, you have to be aware of how it interacts with support or resistance, and what it means when price either breaks through or fails to break through. A failed breakout is most often interpreted as the last thing to occur before prices begin a strong move in the opposite direction. In other words, if sellers try to move price down and fail, it is likely that buyers are going to gain momentum and successfully move price higher, and vice versa. This interaction between sellers and buyers is constant and unending, and every trend eventually loses momentum and turns.

### Key Point

A "rule of opposite movement" applies consistently to trading patterns. After a failure to break through one side, prices invariably move in the opposite direction.

These trading range borders also can be defined as the locations where supply and demand are tested and determined, at least within the moment. No current trading range, no matter how firmly held, is going to be permanent. Stock prices are dynamic and will eventually move away from the trading range, either up or down. From the supply and demand side, the forces affecting prices as well as the trading range borders are clearly defined.

When more traders want to buy, prices are driven up due to more demand than supply; when more sellers want to sell, prices are driven down due to more supply than demand. This oversimplifies the process in a sense, because many influences affect prices beyond the simple forces of supply and demand. These forces include momentary perceptions of value, opinions about a company, earnings reports versus analysts' estimates, mergers and acquisitions, rumors, lawsuits, product recalls or new product announcements, changes in management, and any other important change or belief about a coming change within a company.

Support is the bottom of the trading range. But more specifically, it is the price level where further decline is unlikely, where buyers consider the price attractive and also where sellers are willing to make trades. Below that level, demand becomes too strong for prices to continue downward because buyers perceive the support level as a good price and anything below that would be a bargain. Demand offsets and even surpasses supply at the support level, which prevents further price decline.

If prices do fall below support, it means that sellers have prevailed. Selling expectations are lower and buyers are not interested, perhaps due to weaker than expected earnings, the perception that the stock is priced too high, or a cyclical negative opinion about the industry that comes from economic change. However, support levels rarely go into a freefall except in a market panic. At some point, the price is going to become cheap enough that buyers will once again want to buy shares. That point sets a new level of support.

**support zone**
a range of prices representing support, used in place of a single price.

Because prices may trade briefly below the established support price, traders acknowledge a *support zone* in place of a specific price. This is done because prices may dip below support temporarily. On a candlestick chart, you often see a closing price at or above support, but with the session's trading below that level. This "testing of the waters" below support may come from an attempted bearish breakout, or simply as a momentary trading glitch that does not last.

Resistance is the opposite of support, or the top of the current trading range. It is the price at which prices are not likely to rise any farther because buyers lack the momentum; put another way, sellers consider the resistance price to be acceptable, but anything above that price would be an inflated value. And so resistance holds for the moment as an agreed-upon price. Buyers are not willing to pay more per share than the resistance price.

Putting this in supply and demand terms, as price levels rise to resistance, sellers are more likely to sell and take profits, and buyers are less likely to buy because the price is relatively high.

---

### Key Point

To best understand how the trading borders define price movement, they have to be interpreted in terms of how buyers and sellers view specific price levels.

---

**resistance zone**
a range of prices representing resistance, used in place of a single price.

A breakout above resistance may be permanent, in which case a new trading range will be set. Prices will not rise indefinitely; at some point, momentum slows down and a new resistance level is established. A breakout may also fail to hold, and prices will retreat to the established trading range. In those instances where prices are especially volatile at or near resistance, traders may set a *resistance zone* instead of a specific price. This is a small price range where resistance holds, but trading may move above the price briefly.

The nature and volatility of trading within the trading range often define the strength or weakness of the current resistance and support levels. The trading that takes place within the defined range is called the *channel.* This price movement may remain in a small range or bounce off of both resistance and support while remaining within the borders.

**channel**
trading within the bounds of resistance and support, which does not break through on either side.

When the channels continue in a sideways pattern for an extended period of time, it indicates that the forces of supply and demand (between buyers and sellers) are evenly matched.

The trading range can be firmly set with fixed price levels, and with trading taking place within that range; or it may be dynamic. In a dynamic trading range, the channel moves either upward or downward and both resistance and support rise or fall. However, the breadth remains approximately the same. So the range is defined by its breadth rather than by a fixed price at the top or at the bottom.

## Key Point

The trading range is not always fixed in terms of fixed prices; it can also be represented by a trend upward or downward, but with approximately the same fixed breadth.

An example of a sideways-moving channel was seen in the three-month chart for IBM shown in Figure 9.3.

This channel ends in a pattern seen a lot. Prices break the sideways movement by trending upward, but very quickly prices retreat and end up falling below the channel. This type of price movement is uncertain, but one strong clue about the impending downtrend is found in the fifth and sixth sessions after the breakout. The white real body followed by the longer black real body is a bearish engulfing pattern. Although it takes several more sessions for the trend to actually turn, for IBM this signaled that an uptrend was not going to last.

The channel may also trend upward, as in the case of Caterpillar, shown in Figure 9.4. In this chart, the breadth is quite narrow, about four points from top to bottom, but the trend is clearly upward for about two months. The price rose from the mid-50s to the low 70s in this time period without any change in the breadth.

In a downward-trending channel, the same observation can be made. In the case of the U.S. Oil Fund ETF, which is shown in Figure 9.5, a downward channel moved quickly but the breadth remained at about three points.

**FIGURE 9.3**   Channels, sideways movement.

Chart courtesy of StockCharts.com.

**FIGURE 9.4**   Channels, upward movement.

Chart courtesy of StockCharts.com.

**FIGURE 9.5**   Channels, downward movement.
Chart courtesy of StockCharts.com.

Channels are valuable because they allow you to observe the strict and often narrow breadth of the trading range even in periods when prices are trending. These examples prove that it is possible to witness a strong uptrend or downtrend while continuing to observe the limitations of a dynamic trading range.

# Popular Price Patterns and Their Meaning

The trading range of a stock provides order and the basis for testing potential later price movement. Following are some of the most popular and useful technical patterns and trends used by traders.

> ### Key Point
>
> The head-and-shoulders pattern is a reliable one because it involves a three-part failed test of resistance. This is most likely to lead to a decline after the pattern develops.

The *head and shoulders* is a very well-known and often-observed pattern. It contains three price spikes. The first and third (shoulders) are lower than the

**head and shoulders**

a pattern in chart analysis consisting of three price spikes. The first and third (shoulders) are lower than the second (head). After the failed attempt at driving prices upward, price is expected to react by trending downward after the head and shoulders.

middle (head), and the head is a test of an upward movement. However, because all three spikes retreat, the price is expected to then trend lower. So the three-part test of upward movement fails.

For example, the chart for Boeing in Figure 9.6 shows a head-and-shoulders pattern testing the resistance level of about $73.50 (shoulders) and a very brief breakout (the head). After this, the price falls strongly.

A head and shoulders is usually going to test resistance without breaking through. In this case, the assumed resistance was broken very briefly, and that failed breakout added to the downward momentum in the reaction trend that followed.

An opposite pattern is the *reverse head and shoulders*, which is identical except that the spikes approach or pass support in an attempt to drive prices downward, and the reaction is for prices to trend upward.

An example of the reverse head and shoulders occurred in the three-month chart of Yahoo! shown in Figure 9.7. In this case, the pattern developed after a brief and weak uptrend. The reverse head and shoulders

**FIGURE 9.6** Head and shoulders.
Chart courtesy of StockCharts.com.

**FIGURE 9.7** Reverse head and shoulders.
Chart courtesy of StockCharts.com.

acted just as expected, with prices then breaking into an uptrend that moved strongly for more than two weeks.

These patterns do not have to be perfect or even especially strong for their meaning to provide good signals. With all indicators, the stronger the pattern, the better the information it provides. However, in these examples of the head-and-shoulders pattern—which involves three separate price spikes—even a relatively weak pattern is worth observing, especially if it is also confirmed by other indicators.

> **reverse head and shoulders**
> a chart pattern involving three bottom price spikes. The first and third (reverse shoulders) are not as low as the second (the head). After the failed downward movement, prices are expected to reverse and trend upward.

**Key Point**

> Any technical pattern may vary in its strength or weakness. It is a mistake to wait for a "perfect" or classic example, when a relatively weak pattern has the same significance in predicting price developments.

The Boeing chart (Figure 9.6) includes the very interesting downward-trending day with the long lower shadow as the third in four downward-moving days, then a gap, and then an upward movement. This volatility can be unsettling; however, as the final leg of the head-and-shoulders pattern emerged, the likelihood of a subsequent downtrend became clear. The long lower shadow and then the gap confirmed the volatility of what was emerging. But would that be upward or downward volatility? The head-and-shoulders pattern decided this convincingly.

The reverse pattern for Yahoo! (Figure 9.7) was even weaker, but the strong uptrend that followed conformed to expectations after the reverse pattern was completed. The uptrend was rapid and, as later events showed, could not be held. After it peaked, two events occurred. First was the very large gap between two downtrend days. Second was the volume spike that followed immediately. This revealed that the uptrend had lost momentum and had reversed. A similar event was found at the bottom of the downtrend: a large gap as the downtrend turned into yet another uptrend.

The whole pattern of short-term trends and confirmed reversals involves constant testing of resistance and support. Review charts over several months to spot how these borders hold their importance even long after interim trends have developed and ended.

**double top**
a technical pattern in which price rises to the resistance level twice without breaking through permanently, and after this prices are expected to decline.

Beyond the valuable head-and-shoulders pattern are additional patterns that test resistance and support. A variation of testing resistance is the *double top*. In this formation, prices test resistance twice and then retreat in the opposite direction. The double top is an especially strong bearish development because it demonstrates the significance of resistance when it holds; price not only backs away but tends to fall dramatically after the double top.

The double top may occur after an uptrend or at the conclusion of a sideways movement. For example, as shown in Figure 9.8, Ford saw a double top after an uptrend, and in the middle, prices retreated before rising again. However, after the second attempt at further upward movement, prices retreated strongly.

The opposite pattern is the *double bottom*, which involves two tests of support followed by a reversal and an uptrend. This occurs either after a downtrend or during a sideways movement when buyers and sellers are struggling for control.

### Key Point

Double tops and bottoms are good ways to spot failed breakout attempts, and to anticipate price movement in the opposite direction.

**FIGURE 9.8** Double top.
Chart courtesy of StockCharts.com.

Microsoft's chart showed an example of this, as seen in Figure 9.9. After the double bottom, prices rose but could not be sustained. Price levels finally retreated once again to the level before the double bottom occurred.

Technical analysis is all about patterns, as the head and shoulders and double tops/bottoms reveal. However, it is not only the price level that holds significance to traders, but changes in the breadth of the trading range itself. When the breadth narrows over a series of sessions, it provides a clue of a coming reversal. So the *triangle* is a pattern of declining breadth, and it should not be ignored.

When you see an *ascending triangle*, which occurs during an uptrend, it often means a reversal will occur when the breadth reaches a very narrow point. It consists of flat resistance and rising support.

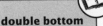

**double bottom**
a technical pattern consisting of two downward price spikes testing support. The failure to break through precedes a reversal and an uptrend after the double attempt.

DuPont's chart included an example of an ascending triangle lasting about one month, and this is shown in Figure 9.10.

This pattern ends with an exceptionally strong bearish engulfing pattern at the very top of the trend. The combination of the triangle and the engulfing pattern confirms the reversal, which occurred immediately after this development.

**FIGURE 9.9** Double bottom.

Chart courtesy of StockCharts.com.

**FIGURE 9.10** Ascending triangle.

Chart courtesy of StockCharts.com.

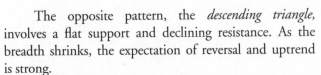

### Key Point

Confirmation vastly improves a trader's accuracy in predictive analysis. For example, when a triangle occurs along with an engulfing pattern, those are two strong clues that prices are going to reverse.

**triangle**
a trend involving changes in the breadth of the trading range. As the range narrows during the current trend direction, the likelihood of reversal increases.

The opposite pattern, the *descending triangle,* involves a flat support and declining resistance. As the breadth shrinks, the expectation of reversal and uptrend is strong.

An example was seen in the case of Verizon, as shown in Figure 9.11. This gradually declining breadth was typical of a pattern taking place just before reversal and an uptrend.

## Trend Lines for Spotting Reversals

To spot and identify a reversal point, or to confirm that reversal is about to occur, the *trend line* is a very valuable and important technical tool. This is a

**FIGURE 9.11** Descending triangle.
Chart courtesy of StockCharts.com.

**ascending triangle**

a pattern of narrowing breadth in the trading range, consisting of flat resistance and rising support, and preceding a likely reversal and downtrend.

straight line drawn underneath rising support, or above falling resistance. When price turns and interrupts the line, it indicates that a reversal has begun.

### Key Point

Trend lines are valuable because they are simple, easy to spot, and provide a clear signal that a trend has ended.

An example of a trend line occurring during an uptrend was seen in the case of McDonalds, shown in Figure 9.12. Prices continued moving upward strongly for two months. The trend line, drawn beneath the rising support, showed exactly where the uptrend ended and reversed.

The opposite trend line, tracking falling resistance levels in a downtrend, is just as easy to spot and just as strong in locating or confirming a reversal and then a subsequent uptrend. For example, the chart for Citigroup, as shown in Figure 9.13, tracked a 20 percent price decline from about $5 down to below $4.

**FIGURE 9.12** Trend line, uptrend.
Chart courtesy of StockCharts.com.

**FIGURE 9.13** Trend line: downtrend.
Chart courtesy of StockCharts.com.

The trend line is a strong indicator and it is easy to develop and follow. This makes it one of the best indicators around. The combination of clarity and simplicity is difficult to beat. Trend lines confirm what other indicators also seem to indicate in reversal patterns.

## Breakouts and Gaps

When price levels move above resistance or below support, the change is significant. However, a momentary breakout can also retreat back into the previous trading range, meaning that the breakout fails. When a breakout is accompanied by a gap, the chances of its reversing and filling are quite high. It's all a matter of momentum. If prices move too high too fast, you have to expect a reversal.

> **descending triangle**
> a bullish sign involving flat support and declining resistance. As the breadth shrinks to a very narrow point, the expectation is for a reversal and uptrend to follow.

> **Key Point**
>
> Both breakouts and gaps can be very meaningful. But when they occur together, smart traders know they have to pay close attention to price movement.

**trend line**
a straight line drawn beneath a rising support level or above a falling resistance level. Once price levels reverse and interrupt the line, a reversal may be indicated or confirmed.

**common gap**
a price gap occurring as a part of normal trading activity and without any signal value for changes in the existing trend.

When the breakout moves above resistance, many changes can occur. For example, in Figure 9.14, Toll Brothers stock broke through resistance; if you began to analyze the price pattern based on the previously mentioned concept of old resistance becoming new support, that level was tested almost immediately.

The price fell after this, so that the breakout failed. In this case, you would not have needed to wait very long to discover that prices were not necessarily on the move, and that the breakout lasted only a few sessions.

The same conditions prevail when a breakout takes price down below support. For example, ExxonMobil experienced a bottom-side breakout in its three-month chart, as shown in Figure 9.15.

This breakout held. After a sideways movement of considerable time, the breakout was followed by a fairly strong downward price trend with no reversal or retesting of the previous level.

Breakouts are revealing, especially when they occur as part of a gapping action. Several gaps were present on Eastman Kodak's chart, including the first one that occurred along with a breakout above resistance, as shown in Figure 9.16.

**FIGURE 9.14** Breakout above resistance.
Chart courtesy of StockCharts.com.

**FIGURE 9.15** Breakout below support.

Chart courtesy of StockCharts.com.

**FIGURE 9.16** Gaps.

Chart courtesy of StockCharts.com.

**breakaway gap**
a type of gap
that moves
prices above or
below the trading
range and either
begins a rally or
retreats back to
the previous level
in subsequent
sessions.

This first gap is not obvious because there was no space in between sessions. However, if you see that the first of the two days was black, meaning it closed at the bottom of the rectangle, then the opening of the next day gapped above that level. This set off what turned out to be a very strong breakout and uptrend.

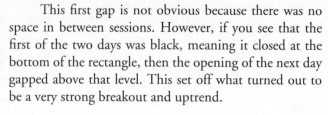

### Key Point

Not all gaps are visible. Detailed analysis reveals that some of the most important gapping patterns involve gaps between up and down days, and these may be shielded because candlestick real bodies overlap.

**runaway gap**
a pattern of
gapping action
involving several
sessions in close
proximity, as
part of a trend
moving strongly
in one direction
without
offsetting price
movement.

The second gap was also subtle. The small distance between the first day's close and the second day's open gave a brief upward indicator. But as the third, strong gap proved, the momentum was not strong enough for this uptrend to last very long. Prices fell quickly, ending up within the range below the original resistance level at the beginning of the chart.

Gaps occur often in most charts. The gap that simply occurs as a matter of normal trading but without any special signal attached is called a *common gap*.

Gaps are important in many different ways. The *breakaway gap* can be subtle and small like the one in the previous chart, or it can be very strong and wide. Its characteristic is that it moves price away from the established trading range.

**exhaustion gap**
a gap occurring
at the end
of a trend,
signifying a loss
of momentum
and a reversal in
price direction.

When a rally takes off strongly, it is also likely to exhaust more quickly. This is not always the case, but on average you may expect to see a quick rally turn suddenly. This is especially true when the trend is accompanied by the *runaway gap* pattern. This is a recurring series of gaps, including consecutive gaps in two or more sessions. This is troubling because of the singular movement without slowing down, and the gapping action may drive price levels much higher or lower than the level justified by actual buyer or seller interest.

> ### Key Point
>
> The runaway gap pattern can be encouraging if prices are going in the direction you want. However, they also mean that the trend is likely to lose momentum quickly and reverse more strongly than trends without these gaps.

**moving average (MA)**
the average price over a fixed number of sessions, adjusted for each new session by removing the oldest and replacing it with the newest day and then dividing the total by the total number of days.

Another kind of gap is called the *exhaustion gap*, and this is found at the end of a trend. After a particularly strong trend with a pattern of runaway gaps, exhaustion gaps are more likelyv than in other trends, and may be seen right as the price direction has turned.

The many types of popular price patterns are valuable not so much by themselves but as part of a greater pattern *and* assuming that two or more indicators confirm the apparent significance of current price positions.

Beyond price patterns tracked over a series of sessions, more advanced indicators provide additional confirmation (or contradiction) and provide greater insight. These enable you to anticipate reversals before most traders know they are going to occur.

**exponential moving average (EMA)**
a formula for weighted moving average, used to provide great impact to the latest entries on a stock price chart.

## Moving Averages, Oscillators, and Volume Tests

Advanced technical indicators include dozens of tests that demonstrate momentum levels and anticipate changes. Among these is the *moving average (MA)* of price.

MA is nothing more than the average price over a fixed number of sessions. For example, if you use a 20-day moving average, it consists of the last 20 days added together and then divided by 20. Tomorrow, the oldest day is removed and the newest day added in and the average is recalculated.

**oscillator**
technical indicators that track price movement and identify overbought or oversold conditions. These aid in picking the best entry and exit points in trades.

**Chaikin Money Flow (CMF)**
an oscillator that identifies overbought or oversold conditions through a mathematical analysis of price trends.

**accumulation/ distribution line**
an analysis of volume in relation to price, based on the CMF theory and stating that volume trends precede price movement.

**Relative Strength Index (RSI)**
an oscillator that tracks upward and downward sessions and compares them to quantify momentum and provide an estimate of overbought or oversold conditions.

### Key Point

Moving averages help spot true trends, whereas short-term price patterns may be chaotic and less reliable.

The calculation becomes cumbersome for longer-span MA like the popular 200-day moving average. Fortunately, with online free charting, MA is easily added into charts instantly and without the need to perform any math.

MA's purpose is to remove the short-term volatility from the price trend and to show how the average price trend is evolving over time. This is most valuable when the MA is below or above current price and remains there as the current trend moves forward, and the trigger for action takes place when price and MA cross over.

To make MA even more valuable, it helps to weight the latest days on the theory that more recent portions of the period are more relevant than the older days. The most popular weighting formula is called *exponential moving average (EMA)*. This is a formula built into online charts to adjust MA to weight the most recent entries.

The most popular MA-based formula is called MACD, which is an abbreviation of "Moving average convergence/divergence." This daunting title simply refers to the analysis of two separate moving average lines, how they relate to price levels, and how the two move closer together or farther apart.

These relationships—breadth between averages and price or between the two averages—help to anticipate a coming price reversal. And as the two lines converge and then cross, or diverge and move farther apart, technicians interpret the changes in terms of how they affect momentum.

### Key Point

The trends you spot in changing moving averages are extremely valuable. By the time the lines cross, most traders already know a reversal has taken place, so the smart move is to spot a coming reversal before everyone else acts.

MA analysis is valuable because it serves as a reliable method of confirming chart patterns or candlestick indicators. Beyond MA, you may use dozens of more advanced indicators. These are broadly called *oscillators*. These are indicators that track trends in order to identify when a stock is either overbought or oversold. When oscillators reach extreme levels on either side, they act as signals. Traders rely on oscillators to find entry and exit points.

Following are two of the most widely used. First is the *Chaikin Money Flow (CMF)*. This is an indicator that calculates when buying or selling pressure reaches a point of extreme, when traders should sell (overbought) or buy (oversold).

The CMF summarizes the *accumulation/distribution line,* which is based on the theory that volume tends to increase before a stock's price moves. So it tracks this trend and identifies positive or negative money flow (volume flow).

A second valuable oscillator is the *Relative Strength Index (RSI)*. This is an analysis of momentum that compares recent upward and downward movements in the stock and uses averages of up days and down days to calculate a single value showing traders the strength or weakness of price at current levels.

These more technical indicators may involve complex mathematical calculations. Fortunately, you need only understand the concept behind the calculation in order to use it. Online free charting services calculate numerous oscillators for you and add them to charts as additional charting segments or color-coded overlays along with the latest price information.

### Key Point

Online free charting has opened up a broad range of complex technical indicators to everyone. However, it is important to understand what is being calculated before making trading decisions based on how those indicators change.

Trading is made more efficient with the Internet, but also more complicated. The wealth of information is valuable, but the volume of information may be counterproductive. For this reason, it makes sense to pick a short list of indicators you believe provide the most reliable initial and confirming information, and track those indicators. If trading direction is uncertain, you can also add in additional indicators if that helps; but start out with fewer rather than with more.

The next chapter concludes the trading section by providing background on some of the technical theories that form the trading philosophy used by so many people and institutions. It is always valuable to know the basic theories and how they are applied. However, at the same time, it is important to remember the distinction between theory and practice.

# Chapter 10

# Technical Analysis, Dow Theory, and Practice

The basis for technical analysis is found in a few principles and theories that deal with price behavior. In other words, prices move for specific reasons, some beyond the economic observations of supply and demand. So beyond the economic reasons for price movement, some ideas have been offered to explain price movement as either efficient or random.

An analysis of market behavior demonstrates, however, that price movement is neither efficient nor random. It is inefficient in the short term primarily because prices tend to overreact to all current and new information and then to correct later. For example, when earnings exceed expectations, right after the announcement is made the stock price might move way ahead of what seems justified. In the following session or two, the surge is corrected and prices retreat. This is not efficient.

**Key Point**

Contrary to popular theories, the stock market is neither efficient nor random. It is a risky venture to buy and sell shares of stock due to the unknown forces that drive prices upward or downward.

Prices cannot be justified as random, either. If prices were random, the "cause and effect" of news and price movement would not be consistent by any measure. However, when good news is released, prices tend to rise; and when bad news is released, prices tend to fall. Furthermore, prices overall tend to follow market averages. So when there is a big price surge or a big price drop, a majority of listed stocks tend to move in the same direction as the big index stocks. This is not random; in fact, it is highly predictable.

# The Efficient Market

The first interesting theory about price behavior is called the *efficient market theory (EMT)*. This theory states simply that prices react to changes in the company, in the market as a whole, and in the economy; and that the current price of stock has already been adjusted for all known information about that company.

The EMT is cynical because it concludes that analyzing a company's financial reports or studying stock charts is meaningless. Since all prices are fair and efficient because the "smart" investors have already bid prices to their proper levels, there is never a discrepancy between price and value.

| **Key Point** |
| --- |
| The efficient market theory cynically states that you cannot make informed selections based on analysis; most investors and traders instinctively know that analysis is the key to profits. |

EMT is controversial and it has many proponents. However, it is flawed for at least three reasons:

**efficient market theory (EMT)**
a belief that the price of stock reflects all known information about the company at all times, and changes rationally, based on new information as it becomes available.

1. *There are no consistently "smart" investors.* In spite of what the academic theory claims, there are no smart investors out there, at least not enough of them. Truthfully, no investors are consistently able to produce profits by their analysis and decisions. If they were, then the efficient market theory might make sense.

2. *Short-term price movement is demonstrably inefficient.* When you study the cause and effect between news about a company and its stock price behavior, you immediately realize that volatility is more important than news and information. Perhaps actual economic and financial news *should* be more important, but the simple truth is that prices behave irrationally. An alternative, the *inefficient* market theory, makes

more sense. EMT is really nothing more than wishful thinking. In a perfect world, the markets—like everything else—would be rational, behave predictably, and make sense. But the truly interesting thing about investing or trading in the market is its volatility and unpredictability.

3. *Short-term fads and trends contradict the tidy theory behind EMT.* If you look back over the history of the stock market, you realize that the driving forces behind big price movements have often been irrational, short-lived, and highly inefficient. For example, the well-known dot.com bubble between 1995 and 2000 was characterized by rapid growth in the value of Internet stocks, followed by an equally rapid price decline. Why? The trend was driven largely by speculation but with no tangible support. The price growth grew from a belief that companies could grow based on future product or service development even though they currently had nothing of value to offer. Initial public offerings were made for companies that did not even have products. The speculative craze ended very suddenly (and inefficiently) in 2000 once the speculative phase was exhausted.

Figure 10.1 shows how the NASDAQ Composite fell in the three years off the dot.com high. It took that long for the index to begin an upward climb, back to about the 2,400 level by mid-2010. NASDAQ is the exchange on which most IT stocks are listed and was the major exchange hit by the dot.com decline.

**Key Point**

Fads like the dot.com bubble prove that markets are anything but efficient; they are more prone to emotional and irrational exuberance.

The dot.com occurrence is only a recent example of how markets operate inefficiently. The dot.com craze was irrational because a majority of the Internet companies had no products to bring to the market, and as a result had never reported profits, or even revenues. The entire matter was one of perception about future value. A few well-known companies (like Google, eBay, and Amazon.com) did survive and moved forward to become very successful examples of Internet-based companies. But the relatively small number out of hundreds of dot.com companies makes the point that markets are driven more by enthusiastic perceptions than by actual numbers.

EMT is supported and believed in largely in academic circles, and much less among actual investors. Academic theories are comforting and reliable, but

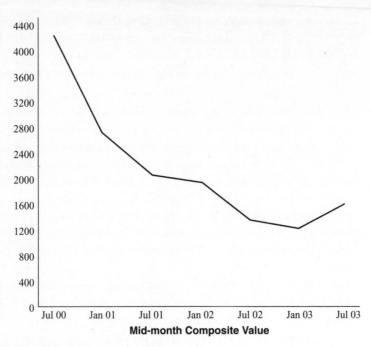

**FIGURE 10.1**   The dot.com decline.
*Source*: NASDAQ.

they remain only theories. No one who has invested capital in the volatile markets of recent years is likely to believe in efficiency as an attribute of the stock market. Actually, being a proponent of EMT is more a matter of faith than of proof. Some observers want the market to be efficient, and so they believe in EMT, even when the evidence shows how inefficient the market truly is. Or, as the successful contrarian Warren Buffett has explained it, "Apparently, a reluctance to recant, and thereby to demystify the priesthood, is not limited to theologians."[1]

# The Random Walk

While EMT suggests that stock is always efficiently priced (and therefore you cannot outperform the market except as a consequence of luck), another theory suggests that price behavior is never based on anything predictable, but is completely random.

---

[1] Warren Buffett, Chairman's Letter to Shareholders, February 28, 1989.

The *random walk theory* is the belief that price behavior cannot be predicted because it does not act on any predictive fundamental or technical indicators. Under the random walk theory, there is an equal chance that a stock's price will either rise or fall from current levels.

The random walk theory contradicts the widely accepted beliefs by both fundamental and technical analysts. Under the theory of fundamental analysis, the long-term value of a company is based on competitive strength, profitability, revenue and market expansion, working capital controls, and capitalization. Under the theory of technical analysis, price is predictable based on chart patterns, momentum indicators, and reversal signals such as those found in candlesticks.

**random walk theory**
a theory stating that stock prices cannot be predicted using any fundamental or technical indicators, because price behavior is entirely random and unpredictable.

---

**Key Point**

The random walk theory is based on a belief that stock prices cannot be predicted, and that all price behavior is the equivalent of a coin flip.

---

Both fundamental and technical analyses have proven to be valuable to investors and traders. Neither system provides 100 percent certainty of profitable decisions or of well-timed entry and exit from positions. However, the analytical tools are intended to improve the timing of decisions, especially for traders relying on a range of technical patterns.

The random walk denies the reliability of any fundamental or technical analysis. It is at least as cynical as the efficient market theory and just as misleading. While short-term markets are clearly chaotic and inefficient, both short-term and long-term pricing can be tied to both fundamental and technical trends. In fact, far from being random, a more supportable belief about price behavior is that fundamental and technical indicators confirm one another, even though the timing is different. In other words, short-term price strength is derived from solid long-term financial strength, and long-term fundamental trends are reflected in the stock's long-term pricing trends as well.

The random walk theory is supported for the most part by academics and some economists, mostly those who rely on theoretical application and mathematical models and less on a study of how invested positions gain or lose value in the real world of the stock market. Those who subscribe to the random walk theory rationalize that prices have to be random because the market is efficient and prices in all currently known facts and influences at each moment. This is illogical, and you can prove this by simply observing the correlation between several forces: earnings news and prices; economic news and economic effects of companies (unemployment, inflation, interest rates, etc.); and changes in sector positions or cyclical movement based on economic change, to name a few.

The theory persists based on academic studies in spite of many developments in analysis, notably free online charting and instant price analysis as a result of the free charting and mathematical tools. The theory has been around for a long time, first introduced in an academic paper by British statistician Maurice Kendall (1953, *The Analytics of Economic Time Series, Part I: Prices*). Two important books expanded on the idea. The first was *The Random Character of Stock Market Prices* (1964) by Professor Paul Cootner. The theory was then expanded upon by Professor Burton Malkiel in *A Random Walk Down Wall Street* (1973).

## Key Point

The flaw in the "proof" of the random walk theory is that price behavior in the market is not the same as a statistical concept. There is a true cause and effect in the market.

These papers and books were well written and thoughtful, but they were based on theory and not on practice. Most investors and traders are better served by relying on fundamental and technical analysis, not so much to ensure profits and eliminate losses, but to improve the ratio between profits and losses based on a rational and serious study of a company's strength and future profit potential (fundamental) and on the strength of the current price as it trends upward or downward (technical).

Some efforts have been undertaken to "prove" the random walk theory by statistical methods. A hypothetical stock's price is predicted based on coin flips, for example, when you know that there is an equal chance of the result being heads or tails. When a series of random coin flips is charted and described as "past performance," proponents of the random walk claim that the pattern can be used to predict future outcomes of coin flipping.

While the random events like coin flips will produce patterns, and those patterns can be interpreted as predictive tools, there is an important distinction between a coin and stock prices. We *know* that the coin flip is random and that all future coin flips are going to be random as well. However, in studying stock price behavior of a company with a known history of a specific volatility level, existing within a specific market sector and with a known competitive position, these known factors certainly affect price movement.

For example, a company with a strong dividend yield, low debt ratio, and consistent record of profits is likely to continue to experience rising prices over time. (If you doubt this, check the 10-year history of Wal-Mart or any other successful and well-managed company that dominates its sector). The reality of the factors influencing stock prices makes the coin flip exercise a statistically inapplicable comparison.

A problem in applying statistical modeling to stock prices, especially to prove the random walk theory, is that coins are not going to behave like stocks. Just because coin flips or any other non–stock price events appear to be random does not mean that stock prices must also be random. Stock price behavior is not random, but is directly influenced by market volatility, financial news, investor and trader perceptions, and dozens of supply-and-demand realities. Just because a stock's price is difficult to predict does not mean it is also random.

The random walk theory conveniently ignores both price trends and momentum. The basic tenet of technical analysis relies on the observed fact that observation of past trends (price direction, momentum, volatility, duration of short-term trends, and more) can be used to predict future price movement. In fact, studies by many market experts provide a strong case to prove that price behavior is not random. Among these tests, a 10-year study by Martin Weber, a behavioral finance researcher, tracked market price changes. Weber found specific patterns that made long-term pricing trends predictable. For example, he found that stocks with upward price patterns and increased earnings tended to outperform other stocks for the following six months.

### Key Point

The problem with the random walk theory is that it ignores the easily observed trends and momentum factors that do directly affect price movement.

Another challenge to the random walk theory was published by Professors Andrew W. Lo and Archie Craig MacKinley (1999, *A Non-Random Walk Down Wall Street*). In this book, a series of tests demonstrated that at least some degree of predictability is present in stocks based on a comparison between price behavior and other influences (earnings, for example). The same authors wrote a paper (2005, "The Adaptive Market Hypothesis") in which financial activity (price behavior) is influenced not randomly, but by the same factors affecting evolution (competition, adaptation, and natural selection).

This is an intriguing concept, because all of these evolutionary concepts also affect a company's ability to survive. Failure to compete (due to obsolete products or better-capitalized competitors), failure to adapt (developing new products as new technology or markets emerge), or the forces of natural selection (the market's preference for one company over another due to any number of reasons) are all interesting. These describe what happens to species in nature as well as to companies in the market.

One of the authors of this paper, Lo, explained this: "Prices reflect as much information as dictated by the combination of environmental conditions and the number of 'species' in the economy."

Within any cyclical period, a stock's price movement can appear very random; this does not prove that all prices act randomly at all times. The environmental model makes this point. If a number of animals in one isolated region starve to death and die out because there is no food, it does not prove that a species goes extinct by random selection. Other animals of the same species are likely to thrive elsewhere and even when one species does go extinct, there are usually logical reasons. Some may be hunted into extinction, while others fail to adapt to their environment or run up against the introduction of new competing species. Some may die out for no apparent logical reason, which also fails to prove that evolution is random.

## Charles Dow and His Market Theory

Charles Dow (1851–1902) wrote a series of editorials in his financial publication, *The Customer's Afternoon Letter*, a two-page summary of each day's financial news that in 1889 was renamed the *Wall Street Journal*. Dow had met his future business partner Edward Jones while the two worked together on the *Providence Evening Press* in Rhode Island. The two men also devised an index they called the Dow Jones Stock Average, which consisted of 11 companies (nine railroads, one steamship company, and Western Union).

**price-weighted average**
a kind of stock market average in which the prices of components are added together and divided by the number of stocks used; the result is that higher-priced stocks have more influence on the average than lower-priced stocks.

### Key Point

The Dow Jones Industrial Average grew out of an attempt by Charles Dow to find reliable business trends.

In 1896, Dow created a new index of 12 stocks. He added their prices together and divided by 12 to arrive at a simple price average. Today, index averaging is normally done in two ways. A *price-weighted average* like the best-known one, the *Dow Jones Industrial Average (DJIA)*, consists of 30 industrial companies' stocks. In this kind of averaging method, higher-priced stocks have greater influence on the index than lower-priced stocks.

In the case of the DJIA, as of June 1, 2010, four companies—IBM, 3M, Chevron, and McDonalds—account for more than one-fourth of the total index value of the DJIA.[2]

The second method of developing an index is called the *capitalization-weighted average*. The best-known of these are the S&P 500 and the NASDAQ Composite. Under this method, the components of the index are weighted according to the size of their total capitalization. In these averages, large price movement in higher-capitalization companies has greater influence on the index value than price movement in components with less capitalization.

Charles Dow did not develop his index theory all at once. Originally, his idea was to develop a method for tracking business trends such as earnings, as well as price trends based on price behavior among leading stocks. This concept was later given a name, the *Dow Theory*. Charles Dow himself never used this term, which was formalized after his death. Dow noticed that stock prices tended to move along with other, broader business trends like growth of the economy, for example. He identified business cycles as important influences on price behavior.

The first person to use the term "Dow Theory" was S. A. Nelson in his 1903 book, *The ABC of Stock Speculation*.

**Dow Jones Industrial Average (DJIA)**
a price-weighted average of 30 blue-chip industrial stocks, popularly used to judge the trend and strength or weakness of the stock market.

**capitalization-weighted average**
a stock market average in which components are weighted according to their market capitalization rather than by price per share.

---

### Key Point

The Dow Theory provides a framework for identifying and quantifying market-wide trends.

**Dow Theory**
a belief in trends set within the markets, based on the original beliefs and observations expressed by Charles Dow.

There are six specific tenets that make up the Dow Theory as developed by William P. Hamilton, fourth

---

[2] IBM = 9.37%; 3M = 5.89%; Chevron = 5.45%; and McDonalds = 5.00%.
*Source:* The Dow Jones Companies, June 1, 2010.

**primary trend**
the overall direction of the market, either bullish or bearish, that lasts from a few months to several years.

**secondary trend**
a trend lasting from a few days to a few months, with prices moving counter to the direction of the primary trend.

**minor trend**
a price trend of only a few days, moving either upward or downward.

**accumulation phase**
the first phase of a trend, during which contrarians and experienced investors and traders buy (in an uptrend) or sell (in a downtrend).

editor of the *Wall Street Journal*, who actually developed and refined the theory:

1. *Markets consist of three levels of price movement, or trends.* Price behavior consists of a *primary trend*, a period when the direction—upward or downward— is clearly established and lasts between several months and several years. The *secondary trend* is a movement in the direction opposite the primary trend, in which price levels retrace the primary movement between 33 percent and 66 percent, and that lasts from a few days to a few months. The *minor trend* is the movement of only a few days, which may move in either direction.

2. *Trends all contain three specific stages.* Every trend is made up of three distinct parts. These are predictable and exact. First is the *accumulation phase*, a period in which contrarian and experienced investors and traders buy shares (during an uptrend) or sell shares (during a downtrend). This often occurs when over- all market sentiment is to do the opposite. Second is the *public participation phase*, a period in which the market follows the early lead introduced during the accumulation phase, and buying or selling becomes widespread. Third is the *distribution phase*, the period in which those who led accumulation now sell appre- ciated shares or buy depressed shares, marking the last portion of the trend.

3. *All news is discounted.* This rule tells you that the mar- ket absorbs information, which goes into changing the price.

   Some price changes occur even before the news is announced, in anticipation of that news. The "dis- counting" of news and information is also called "effi- ciency" and this rule has been used as a rationalization of the efficient market theory.

4. *Market averages have to confirm one another before a new trend can be identified.* The original theory was based on the importance of the "rails" (later changed to be called "transportation" and to encompass truck- ing, shipping, and airlines). In the time of Charles Dow, the United States was expanding quickly as an

industrial power, and factories needed to ship goods from widely dispersed areas into urban centers. This led to the conclusion that the strength or weakness of the transportation sector dictated the existence or change in a primary trend. Under this rule, today's Dow Theory is based on confirmation between averages. When one average begins moving, it does not represent a new trend until a second average also changes direction, confirming the new trend. For primary trends, the industrial and transportation averages are the most important indicators of trends and changes in trends. Today, the transportation sector continues to offer symptoms of economic health within the economy. The more production and selling, the more goods are moved to markets. So the transportation average is a crucial confirmation tool for industrial trends.

**public participation phase**
the second phase of a trend, in which the market follows the lead of those in the accumulation phase and buys or sells shares in the indicated direction.

5. *Trends in price must be confirmed further by changes in volume of trading.* Dow Theory observers have noted that changes in prices and trends that occur on low volume might be false indicators, or are caused by deceptive actions such as *short covering.* But when price direction changes and volume are also higher than average, that is seen as additional confirmation that the trend is legitimate.

6. *Trends continue in effect until signals establish a clear reversal.* Trends do not simply evaporate or stop without a signal developing to show that something has taken place, often a reversal and the beginning of a new trend in the opposite direction. Short-term price movement is always chaotic, and for this reason Dow Theory observers rely on strong reversal signals, changes in volume, and other technical tools.

**distribution phase**
the third stage in a trend, in which leading investors or traders sell appreciated shares (uptrend) or buy depressed shares (downtrend), marking the end of the trend.

The Dow Theory is not perfect, but it does provide a framework for managing short-term market chaos and identifying longer-term trends. The Dow Theory employs averages, meaning everything is discounted; with this in mind, the indicators are not perfect and everything has to be confirmed.

**short covering**
buying activity resulting from holders of shorted stock closing positions; when short covering occurs at a high volume, it may create an artificially high buy indicator.

### Key Point

All indicated reversals located using the Dow Theory rely specifically on confirmation. This is a requirement before a new trend can be called.

Is the Dow Theory still valid today? With the Internet making market news and information widely and easily accessible, some critics have stated that the Dow Theory is outdated. However, especially for traders who rely on confirmation as a basic tool for timing of entry and exit, the rules governing the Dow Theory apply even in the completely automated age.

The final section of this book presents ideas that help you to combine the elements of investing and trading into a single approach to the markets. A majority of people are going to discover that their philosophy does not fit completely into either a fundamental or a technical belief system, but is more likely to rely on elements of both.

Part

3

# Combining Investing and Trading

# The Contrarian Approach to Trading

Whether you consider yourself an investor or a trader, a second question you need to answer is whether you are going to employ strategies in a contrarian manner.

A contrarian approach is based on the belief that the majority is usually wrong. Accordingly, by buying when everyone else is selling, and selling when everyone else is buying, the logic follows that your experience will be better than average.

This oversimplifies the strategy to a degree. The majority is often wrong, but the belief that most traders are always wrong is not accurate. As a general rule, following the investing and trading crowd is a mistake; by the time a trend or opportunity is recognized by everyone, it has usually passed. In that case, jumping in is a matter of poor timing. Contrarians recognize that most buying activity peaks at the top of an uptrend and most selling appears at the bottom.

**Key Point**

The contrarian is not simply contradictory; he or she just realizes that timing of trade decisions is likely to be wrong.

This is true. It gives profound context to the old advice, "Buy low and sell high." That sounds easy assuming you know where "low" and "high" are located. The contrarian approach is based on the realization that the majority (not everyone, but the majority) tends to do the opposite, to buy high and sell low.

## The Contrarian Concept: Why Go against the Market?

The value of contrarian investing is anything but settled science. It is controversial. If you believe that the market's conventional wisdom is often wrong, then contrarian strategies will be appealing and potentially more profitable than following the crowd beliefs. History, whether of market activity or science, has demonstrated that the consensus is easily wrong more than right. So a contrarian relies on the tendency of the majority to time entry and exit poorly, and for that same majority to follow rather than to lead.

Within the market, contrarian investing and trading is a popular approach but it is not always easy to apply. When prices of a stock are rising rapidly, it is difficult to resist the temptation to jump in and take advantage of the trend. When prices are falling, it is equally difficult to resist the temptation to get out before prices fall even more.

| Key Point |
| --- |
| The hardest part of the contrarian strategy is having the discipline to go against what the majority thinks. |

As a contrarian, you need to put aside the emotional and natural impulses to act in the same manner as everyone else, and to be willing to sell when prices have risen too quickly or buy when prices have declined and when everyone else is fearful.

This is counterintuitive to the way that most people naturally think and act. This is due to what most people perceive about how to act either individually or collectively. As social beings, people know that collective action is powerful and convincing. This has both positive and negative aspects for investors and traders. If the crowd psychology of the market is to believe that a company is going to grow rapidly, then the collective demand for stock will drive up prices. But how far will that go? If you are one of the early believers in this supply-and-demand trend, then you can profit well from taking up positions. However, at some point the crowd psychology can convert into a more mindless form and revert to mob mentality. In this phase, people are likely to act irrationally and take comfort in the collective action itself rather than analyzing the opportunity rationally and logically.

Investors and traders have to overcome crowd psychology in order to act and behave as a contrarian, and it is against human nature to do so. Sigmund Freud wrote that people acting within a crowd majority tend to act differently toward people thinking outside of the crowd's belief. In other words, a majority does not easily accept contradiction offered by individuals. Most people instinctively want to be accepted as part of the crowd, or "tribe" of people thinking alike, in the belief that the collective belief provides safety and protection. However, contrarians are aware that as a crowd's beliefs are made uniform, each individual within the crowd is likely to become less aware of their actions as individuals. It gets easier to go along with the majority.

Whether a crowd becomes a mindless mob with an anonymous and comforting personality, or is simply a group of like-minded individuals, is controversial. No one can identify conclusively why crowds act as they do, but the tendency is a reality. For anyone acting as a contrarian, the most difficult aspect is ignoring the desire to be a part of the crowd.

### Key Point

It is human nature to want to be accepted, which is why most people cannot successfully apply contrarian theories to their timing.

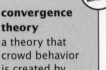

The issue is complex. Under the belief of *convergence theory*, crowd behavior is not an automatic response of crowd thinking, but is created by individuals who bring the thinking into the crowd. This "contagion" grows from a crowd of like-minded people. This makes a certain degree of sense when applied to markets. For example, when several people are prone to believe that a particular stock is likely to increase in value, one influential individual acts by buying stock, and is imitated by others who share the point of view. They converge into thinking in the same manner.

**convergence theory**
a theory that crowd behavior is created by individuals who bring ideas to the crowd, rather than as a spontaneous matter. In the market, individuals who act in a particular way may influence others to follow their behavior.

In convergence theory, an individual who buys or sells shares of stock may influence others based on a shared belief in the conditions of the market, inherent risks or opportunities, or the tendency to go along with people in similar circumstances. So in a work or social setting, a respected investor or trader can hold a great deal of influence over his or her peers and when that individual makes entry or exit decisions, the convergence of thought may easily lead to a duplication of the action.

A contrarian, however, recognizes convergence theory and resists it. The recognition of the tendency gives a contrarian great power, because that contrarian has insight not only into the crowd's mentality to act together, but into *why* the crowd does so.

Putting this another way, a contrarian recognizes how crowd behavior works as a predictable force in the market and is able to exploit it. The convergence of many individuals creates price movement in the market that inevitably creates mispricing. So when there is good news, the price is driven too high and has to correct in subsequent sessions, and on bad news, the crowd drives price lower than the news justifies, meaning the price corrects in the following sessions. This endless overreaction of price is the key to successful swing trading (Chapter 7), but it also points to the short-term advantages that all contrarian traders and investors hold. By not going along with the crowd thinking, they are able to recognize overreaction and act accordingly.

| **Key Point** |
|---|
| Contrarians tend to be astute observers of human behavior, and are able to recognize moments when the majority belief is likely to be wrong. |

This applies not only to the very short-term price swings that occur on a daily basis, but also to longer-term trends. A general belief in a company's potential for growth may lead to exaggerated price appreciation (reflected in the P/E ratio rising quickly, for example), and the same kind of crowd-based belief that a company is not a sound investment may easily depress its stock's value. Both of these conditions create opportunities for contrarian investors.

Contrarians may act on their observations about price movement by buying depressed stock, short-selling stock that is overpriced, or using options on either side to exploit the very short-term price swings that may occur. For long-term investing, the use of price declines to oversold conditions can be used to identify a bargain price level and to buy shares in carefully selected companies. This is a strategy used by value investors. The concept requires prequalifying a company based on a few sound fundamental principles, and then seeking a bargain price as the entry point.

# Contrarians and the Permanent Bear or Bull Mentality

There is an important difference between a bear mentality and the contrarian trader or investor. A trader with a permanent bear mentality believes that market trends are always downward, even in bull markets. While the view is contrarian, it is unyielding. The permanent bear is right only half of the time.

An equally common problem is found in the overly optimistic permanent bull approach. Like the bear, the bull is right only half of the time and during bear markets, the bull trader is acting in a contrarian manner.

A true contrarian is more flexible than either a permanent bear or a permanent bull. The contrarian should constantly be in "evaluation mode" about overall markets as well as individual stocks. All market trends are cyclical, meaning prices rise and prices fall. As a matter of improved timing, a contrarian questions the crowd mentality that follows trends, when timing is invariably improved if you lead rather than follow. A contrarian is not by definition either a bull or a bear, but rather observes the market direction. The key is to identify the direction properly and to note when trading sentiment is moving in the wrong direction. This is most likely to occur at or near the top of uptrends and the bottom of downtrends.

**Key Point**

Unlike the permanent bull or bear, a contrarian recognizes that opportunities are most likely to occur at the top of an uptrend and at the bottom of a downtrend.

The advice to "buy low and sell high" has great significance, but only contrarians are able to act on the advice. Because buying activity accelerates as prices top out, and selling activity accelerates when prices bottom out, contrarians have to be able to step back from the emotional investment in a market position, and to make rational observations. By doing so, timing is vastly improved and the contrarian learns to ignore the human instinct to go along with the majority.

Contrarians belong to neither the bear nor the bull camp because they have specific traits:

- *They are able to think and act independently.* Perhaps the most difficult character trait to develop is thinking independently, especially when the majority holds an opposite view. The independence of thought that contrarians work to create in themselves requires self-discipline and demands that you ignore impulse and gut reaction. The gut reaction that arises when you are tempted to go along with the majority is most likely to occur at the wrong point in the price cycle—to buy at the top and sell at the bottom—and this is where the contrarian philosophy is based.

- *Contrarians are not invested in price direction.* Many traders and investors are personally invested in a fixed belief about the market. Either they are optimistic and believe that prices are always about to turn upward, or they are pessimistic and believe that the market is about to crash. A contrarian refuses to adopt a fixed philosophy or to give into social pressure to act on beliefs that can only be correct for a small period of time.

- *A default assumption is that the majority is more likely to be wrong than to be right.* It is not fair to say that the crowd is *always* wrong, but it is equally false to assume that the crowd is always right. When in doubt, a contrarian will choose to go with the belief that the majority is more often wrong than right. If you track trading volume along with price trends, you often see rises and even spikes in volume right before a price reversal at the end of the trend. In fact, swing traders look for volume spikes as one of the strongest reversal signals, primarily because the majority acts within the crowd mentality, with accelerated buying at the top and selling at the bottom.

## Value Investing and the Contrarian Approach

Distinctions are made between the philosophy of investing and trading (like the contrarian approach) and the kinds of investments themselves (like value or growth investments, for example). However, the contrarian approach contains some elements that make it compatible with value investing.

So you can be a value investor, seeking companies with excellent management, competitive position, and fundamentals, and at the same time act as a contrarian in how and when you buy shares. In a widespread market price decline, for example, many excellent value companies will experience dips in their stock price, which from a value investment point of view is the best time to buy. At such times, though, many investors and traders are fearful of further declines so they do not act.

**Key Point**

Value investors often are also contrarians, because they recognize bargain prices at the moment when most people have an unfavorable view of a company.

Even if a stock's price could fall more, the value investing ideal is to buy shares when they are priced at bargain levels. Even if they decline further, they are still bargains. A mispriced stock is valuable because the market as a whole, with its tendency to exaggerate price movement, has driven the price unreasonably low. Value investors tend to rely on metrics to measure bargain pricing, among which the P/E ratio is prominent. The relationship between market value and *book value* is an additional test. In the most extreme market declines, it is possible for a stock to fall temporarily below reported book value, meaning it is selling at less than the actual net value of the company's balance.

Book value includes intangible assets, so a conservative adjustment to book value is to remove intangible assets and calculate the tangible book value per share. Stock prices rarely fall below a company's book value, but extreme bad news can cause this. The news may relate to the company specifically, to a sector, or to the market as a whole.

A value investor seeks bargain pricing based on the fundamentals and a contrarian looks for price disparity above or below *fair value* to time entry or exit.

The primary difference between value investing and the contrarian philosophy of investing is one of indicators that are used. A value investor relies on the metrics, and a contrarian is more attuned to market sentiment at the moment. The ideal value investment is purchased at a discount from its tangible book value (or from a calculated intrinsic value based on measurements like P/E, for example). The ideal contrarian move takes place whenever a stock's price is well above or below fair value based on sentiment. The common sentiment is either greed on the way up, or fear on the way down; a contrarian exploits the market's tendency to exaggerate these temporary opinions and reactions, buying when everyone else is selling and selling when the "crowd" is buying.

**book value**
the true value of a company based on balance sheet reporting; it is the total of all assets, minus the total of all liabilities. When the net value is divided by outstanding shares, the result is book value per share.

**fair value**
a fundamental indicator intended to value a stock and its growth potential based on a specific measurement; this is compared to the current market value of stock to seek bargain prices.

### Key Point

Value investors rely on fundamental indicators to pick companies, and contrarians rely more on market sentiment and exaggerated price movements.

# Valuable Strategies

A contrarian approach can be as simple as the technical observations of price swings made in a swing trading or day trading strategy, or far more complicated based on volatility indexing or trends in options trading.

> ### Valuable Resource
>
> To learn more about the VIX and how it works, go to www.cboe.com/micro/vix.

The swing approach relies on charting patterns. The most popular among these are the short-term trend, narrow-range day, and volume spike. When these occur along with a clear reversal day, the swing trader defies the popular sentiment and makes a contrarian move. Swing traders are the ultimate technical contrarians.

Measuring volatility is a method preferred by traders who have observed a correlation between market trends and options trading. The Chicago Board Options Exchange Volatility Index (VIX) has been used since 1993 to measure market volatility. It is based on trends in the *implied volatility* of options on stocks in the S&P 500 index.

**implied volatility**
the level of volatility and risk in options trading, comparing current prices of options to established pricing models. The greater the gap between current market value and the pricing model price level, the higher the market volatility.

The VIX is a predictive index often called the "fear index" because it measures market uncertainty. High implied volatility is viewed as a measurement of traders' fears about marketwide trends and the potential for increased risk over the next 30 days.

VIX valuation is derived from weighted price blending for a range of options on stocks of the S&P 500. However, in addition to serving as a measurement of current volatility, the VIX has also become a speculative market instrument in its own right. As of 2006, VIX options contracts were first traded directly; these are literally options on an index tracking options volatility. The VIX also is traded in the futures market and as an ETF that tracks futures performance levels. As a result, traders can speculate on increases or decreases in market risk based on changes in the implied volatility of options.

Before the VIX, an older volatility index, the VXO, was used. This was a calculation of 30-day implied volatility, but only for at-the-money options (the condition when the strike price is identical to market value of the underlying stock).

Because volatility is one of the important elements used to calculate overall premium value of options, using options to measure market volatility makes sense. The broad options market has become an important market indicator as a result. While a segment of the investing and trading world continues to think of options as highly speculative, intangible "side bets" on the market and on direction of price movement, they provide more valuable functions as well. Contrarians with advanced knowledge and experience are likely to track VIX to help time and confirm other indicators to time entry and exit.

| **Key Point** |
| --- |
| The VIX is called the "fear index" because it measures not the volatility of the market, but the perception of volatility. |

Contrarians are aware of the significance of VIX as a "fear index" that can provide valuable insight. Many people view VIX as a specific measurement of volatility, thinking that a high VIX level translates to a bearish stock market. However, this is not the case. A high VIX measures the *fear* of volatility, which can mean the market is perceived as volatile in either a bullish or bearish direction. This distinction is important. The activity in the speculative side of the options market is quantified within the VIX, and this is translated to a percentage value. It is not just the percentage that conclusively determines volatility, but the change in the VIX percentage over time. As the percentage rises, it means the perception of volatility is rising as well. It measures how options traders perceive the market by how willing they are to trade in options over the next 30 days. Likewise, when traders think the risk levels are low, the VIX will fall to reflect that perception.

Contrarians are not limited to the VIX to time their trading decisions. They use a variety of measurements. Among these is a strategy called *dogs of the Dow*. The theory underlying this is that investors tend to pick the 10 DJIA stocks whose dividend is the highest percentage of the current price per share. The theory states that companies offering the highest dividend levels are likely to outperform the overall DJIA stock index.

The dogs of the Dow is so called because higher dividend yield is likely to result from a decline in market price of shares. This occurs because dividends are fixed for the current year even while stock prices move. So when a company's stock price loses value, the dividend

**dogs of the Dow**
a measurement of dividend yield and stock prices, based on the belief that the 10 DJIA stocks with the highest dividends relative to stock price are also likely to outperform the market average.

yield increases. For example, consider what happens to a company that started the year with shares at $50, and declaring a dividend of $1.00 per share. What happens when the stock price falls to $40 per share, or to $30?

| Price per Share | Dividend | Dividend Yield |
|---|---|---|
| $50 | $1.00 | 2.0% |
| $45 | $1.00 | 2.2% |
| $40 | $1.00 | 2.5% |
| $35 | $1.00 | 2.8% |
| $30 | $1.00 | 3.3% |

The lower the price, the higher the yield. According to the contrarian model, the 10 Dow stocks with the highest yield are also most likely to be at the bottom of their price cycle. If this does truly identify stocks that are oversold, it makes sense to go long in the dogs of the Dow. In addition to the benefit of buying at the bottom of the price cycle, the contrarian using this method also gets a higher-than-average dividend yield. In the example above, the stock at $30 per share yields 3.3 percent, but when the same stock was at $50, dividend yield was only 2.0 percent.

### Key Point

Declining stock prices result in higher dividend yield, making a depressed stock more profitable on the dividend side. For contrarians, this can also be used to find bargain-priced stocks.

To critics of the theory, the highest-yielding stocks may also be the most distressed among the 30 industrials. However, the distressed situation may refer only to a price cycle and not necessarily to an economic or business cycle. Because of this, a contrarian may use the dogs as one of several indicators pointing to smart timing, but also check other indicators to avoid buying shares in companies losing their value investment status as well. The dogs of the Dow is also useful in timing of sales. As prices rise and stocks are no longer in the grouping of 10 stocks, it can signal the time to sell. For contrarians, this means selling shares after prices have risen, clearly a contrarian move. At such times, it is more likely that traders will be buying up shares based on strong upward movement.

These 10 stocks are called "dogs" because the bargain pricing and attractive dividend yield appear when the stocks are out of favor. And so contrarians move in and buy at that moment. When the market once again likes those companies (meaning they are no longer dogs), the contrarian takes the change as a sell signal.

# Merging Technical and Fundamental in a Contrarian Strategy

A contrarian does not have to be strictly an investor or a trader. The two philosophies can be merged into a single contrarian strategy. A good way to understand contrarian thinking is to equate it with the tendency within the market for people to (a) act impulsively, (b) overreact to virtually all news, good and bad, and (c) follow rather than lead.

These attributes make a majority of investors and traders more likely to time their decisions poorly. Impulsive behavior includes trading in stock based on today's news, meaning they trade at the "exaggeration point" of the stock's price. For example, an earnings report is released and the reported earnings are far above expectations. As a result, the stock's price jumps by four points. An impulsive decision would be to buy shares right away, in the belief that the good news is only the beginning of a spectacular uptrend. However, a contrarian is going to recognize that the four-point jump is an overreaction to the good news, and that it is likely that the price will decline in coming sessions to a more realistic level, perhaps giving back half of the four-point rise.

| Key Point |
|---|
| Reacting to news, either positive or negative, and trading as a result, means timing is likely to be poor. That news is probably already reflected in the stock's price, so the opportunity has been lost. |

Overreaction to all news works in both directions. The decision to buy on good news or to sell on bad news overlooks an important fact: The news, once known to everyone, is probably already reflected in the current price and, of course, that is likely to be exaggerated. So just as buying after good news means you will probably overpay, selling just after bad news means you are giving up stock at a price that is too low and will probably rebound in the next day or two.

The tendency to follow rather than to lead is very common. Following is easier and it feels safer, but it also means that many trading decisions are going to be made at the worst possible times. It is the primary attribute of the expensive but widespread "buy high and sell low" approach to the market.

Contrarians recognize all of these tendencies, which is why they have a more profitable experience by going against the intuitive or impulsive decisions that most people make. As a group, investors and traders tend to think that the latest trend is a permanent condition. So a stock that has lost value is always going to perform badly, and a stock that has outperformed the market is always going to perform above average. This view of the market is very common; it is also the key to contrarian success. However, to succeed as a contrarian, you have to be able to time trades in exactly the opposite direction of the majority. This means you have to move in when everyone else is fearful, and step back when everyone else is euphoric. This advice is easier to give than to follow, so contrarians are not just good at timing. They also are highly disciplined and able to set and follow rules for themselves that fly in the face of what the majority thinks.

## Contrarian Views in Perspective

The tendency for investors and traders to go along with the crowd mentality is reinforced within the market itself. If you watch financial shows on television, you will notice a tendency to follow the trend. If the market has a huge drop in a single day, featured stories will include "Is this the correction we have been expecting?" or "Is this the start of a bear market?" If the market jumps several hundred points, the opposite features are likely. Stories on topics like "The new bull market" or "The end of the recession" are quite likely. Financial journalism, like all forms of journalism, caters to majority thinking. With this in mind, contrarian thinkers can take a contrarian clue from the financial news programs. It may be wise to act in opposition to journalist "expert" advice.

A cultural tendency is to go along with what most people believe. If most people think the market is going to rise, declaring yourself a bear makes you an outsider and perhaps even an oddity. The nonconformist (another word for contrarian) is shunned and even ridiculed by the majority and their spokespeople. So being a contrarian is not the easiest path, although it is often the most profitable.

> **Key Point**
>
> People tend to want to be accepted, so acting as a contrarian is counterintuitive. Few people seek out nonconformity as a style of behavior, although in the market it may be more profitable.

A true contrarian does not act in a contrary manner for its own sake and will not *always* decide against the majority. There have been many famous market experts who called markets incorrectly and lost all credibility as a result. For example, Joseph Granville was a famous market forecaster in the 1970s and 1980s. Between 1979 and 1981 his predictions in his newsletter (*Granville Market Letter*) were virtually perfect. But that is not what he is remembered for. In 1982, Granville predicted that the market was going to decline significantly. However, the moment of his prediction turned out to be the beginning of one of the strongest historical long-term bull markets. He remained bearish all the way to 1996.

Granville is remembered not for his amazing ability to call market trends between 1979 and 1981, but for his refusal to turn away from his bearish prediction for 15 years of mostly rising markets. This made Granville an object of ridicule despite his record of past successes. It also gave contrarian investing a black eye. If Granville was the ultimate contrarian from 1981 to 1996 by insisting a bear market was on the horizon, then contrary investing is simply a form of inflexibility.

This was not a typical contrarian story. In fact, Granville's reputation as a permanent bear even in a long-term bull market is contradicted by the principles of contrarian investing. Because he was so invested in being right about his bearish call, he refused to pay attention to subsequent signals. A true contrarian would be able to get over a poorly timed call and start fresh by analyzing the current market based on what the signs provided.

With the many attributes of contrarian investing (buying at bargain price levels or preferring to go against the majority, for example), the real meaning of the strategy is more. A contrarian does not simply defy the majority, but is analytical in how the majority thinking gets interpreted. The consensus view should always be suspect, and there is great historical precedent for this. In science, for example, many of the greatest advances have been made by individuals willing to go against the majority. A famous example is that of Galileo, who proved through observation that the earth rotated around the sun and not the other way around. The power of the day, the Church in Rome, threatened Galileo through the Inquisition because his beliefs contradicted biblical passages. Galileo was a scientific contrarian who was forced to retract his claims under threat of death and ended his life in house arrest. Yet his views were correct, even though contrary to the commonly held beliefs of the day.

The same reality applies in the market, though with less severe consequences than those Galileo faced. For investors and traders, taking on the majority is daunting. However, a successful contrarian is also likely to be more analytical and methodical than the typical investor. Most people are simply impulsive and act too quickly and on too little hard evidence. A contrarian might end up drawing the same conclusion or a different one, but the real meaning of contrary investing is not "doing the opposite" in each and every case. Its most profound application is in the tendency to review the evidence carefully before making a trade. So it is contrary to act after studying the facts rather than to jump aboard because the majority has made a decision. Most noncontrarians will make fast decisions because they fear losing an opportunity (to get in before prices go higher or to get out before they go lower). A contrarian refuses to act quickly just because that is what almost everyone else is doing.

**Key Point**

History is full of examples of contrarians being shunned, and even imprisoned or worse. This bolsters the human tendency to want to remain silent and go along with the crowd.

This raises an interesting rhetorical question: If contrary investing and trading makes such sense, why isn't everyone a contrarian? This is a paradox, of course, because if everyone acted as a contrarian, it would create a new herd mentality.

There is a greater reason for most people not to act as contrarians. It comes down to the question of conformity and fear. Most people know that it is a very uncomfortable matter to act contrary to the majority and also to be proven wrong. This fear is a compelling force for most people, causing them to prefer the illusion of safety in the crowd to the potential for profitability by acting in the opposite manner. The social belief that the majority is always right is such a democratic ideal that it becomes accepted truth, even when in fact the majority is simply wrong. A contrarian in a democratic society is a minority, a troublemaker, or even an eccentric.

People also tend not to act as contrarians because they want the efficient market theory to be true. Investors and traders are continually seeking certainty in the market, even though the market by definition is very uncertain (and inefficient). If the majority acts in a particular way, it must be in response to efficiency within the market. In other words, a stock will rise or fall because the majority believes it. A contrarian recognizes that group thinking does not create (or even respond to) efficiency, but tends to disprove the efficient market theory. This is ironic because it defies logic. If there were such a thing as an efficient market, it would be a relatively easy matter to buy and sell at the right moment, because emerging trends would be obvious. Lacking this efficiency, investors and traders tend to substitute majority opinion for what they seek, and to assume that the majority opinion is in fact a reflection of market efficiency.

A contrarian approach works well for individuals, given all of the complexities of timing investment and trading decisions. The conclusion most obviously reached is that following the crowd is not a successful method for profiting in the market. Because known information is normally factored into price, reacting to what others do is a poor way to time entry and exit effectively. It is more likely to lead to ill-timed decisions.

Mixing speculation and investing within a contrarian philosophy is one of the best ways to diversify capital, with some capital left to grow in long-term value companies selected with fundamental analysis, and another portion used to play short-term price swings and based on a largely technical approach. Using both forms of analysis and diversifying between speculation and investing is the topic of the next chapter.

# 12

# Mixing Speculation and Investing

The choice between investment and trading strategies does not have to be exclusive. It makes the most sense to combine both approaches in a manner that works for you and best serves your portfolio, conforms to your risk tolerance, and accomplishes the level of control you need and want.

In selecting a company (the fundamental approach) or a stock (the technical approach), you can employ combinations of both fundamental and technical analysis. The goal is to decide which companies work as long-term value investments, and how to time entry and exit into positions in the short term. Both can maximize your profits and minimize your losses if your approach includes as much analytical source material as you need.

A profound realization in using both fundamental and technical analysis is that you eventually find them to be attributes of the same selection process. If you choose to follow only one or the other, you miss valuable indicators concerning a company's profitability and working capital strength, and you also miss the chance to time trades in the best possible manner.

### Key Point

Fundamental and technical analyses are actually not different matters, but attributes of the same cause and effect in stock valuation.

This chapter introduces essential ideas for mixing investment and speculation into a single strategy. This involves developing a program that identifies a short list of indicators from each side; using fundamental indicators like dividend yield as a timing strategy; using combined analysis as a method for diversification; incorporating safe and conservative options strategies into a portfolio management plan; and resolving a changing long-term investment strategy into a short-term trading approach when the change is justified by changing conditions.

## The Fundamental/Technical Combination

For many investors and traders, the choice of a method for selection of stocks and timing is a matter of passionate belief. The true believers in one system are likely to completely ignore the other approach.

A fundamental analyst makes a mistake, however, by ignoring or discounting the valuable intelligence found with technical indicators. Using technical signs to bolster a fundamental program is valuable for several reasons:

- *Confirmation is extremely valuable as a means for judging a company and its overall strength.* Anyone who picks stocks and tries to build a portfolio of safe, strong, competitive companies is continually seeking confirmation, and on several levels. To the technician, confirmation is a brief, momentary signal about the timing of a buy or sell decision. But to a fundamental investor, confirmation has a different meaning. When you develop a short list of potential investments, fundamental indicators can be used to confirm your original assumptions; but this is not always enough. The information you gain from also reviewing some technical indicators (notably those that identify price volatility) can aid you in narrowing down your list.

  The same is true in the ongoing monitoring of companies whose stock is in your portfolio. When should you sell? You continually seek signs that the circumstances (earnings, working capital, competitive strength, dividend yield) continue to make a company appropriate for your portfolio, but conditions change. When fundamental changes occur, technical indicators can confirm (or contradict) what appears to be taking place.

- *Changes in price volatility have fundamental meaning and significance.* Among the technical indicators most important to fundamental investors is the price volatility of stock. Volatility is another word for market risk, and the wider a trading range, the greater that risk. On a long-term basis, you seek strong companies with earnings growth, great working capital, and exceptional management. However, when volatility increases there is always a reason. Technical indicators based on price volatility (such as breakout from previous trading range or expansion of the range's breadth) may serve as an early warning that the company's fundamental position is going through a change as well.

---

### Key Point

Volatility does not change spontaneously or for no reason. It is usually traced back to something changing in the fundamentals.

---

- *Combined indicators are basic tests of fundamental strength.* Most fundamental investors accept the use of the P/E ratio as a good test of how fair a company's stock price is at the moment; this ratio is even more valuable when studied over the long term and as an annual range between high and low P/E. The trend is interesting because it tracks the market's perception of the company and its future growth prospects.

Three additional combined indicators are also worth studying. These are *return on equity (ROE),* return on invested capital (ROIC), and return on assets (ROA).

**return on equity (ROE)** a ratio comparing net return from operations to the value of shareholders' equity, used to measure the effective use of invested capital to generate profits.

ROE is an important expansion of fundamental analysis and comparisons between companies. ROE tests and tracks the trend in how effectively the capital invested by shareholders is used to create profits. To some, this relationship is obscure or indirect; however, it does provide a monitoring ratio that reveals how well the company applies its capital to generate profits. The formula requires dividing net return by shareholders' equity:

$$\text{net return} \div \text{shareholders' equity} = \text{ROE}$$

If equity levels have changed significantly during the year due to new issues of common shares or retirement of previously outstanding shares, an average number of outstanding shares should be used for the year to accurately reflect the relationship.

A second combined ratio is the *return on invested capital (ROIC)*. This is similar to the ROE, but adjusts for dividends paid out during the year. The theory in this ratio is that dividend payments reduce the net return, so using this net is a more accurate indicator than ROE.

The formula for ROIC is:

$$\text{(net return − dividends paid)} \div \text{total capital} = \text{ROIC}$$

This formula is also called return on capital. A variation of the formula calculates "total capital" to mean "total capitalization," in which case the long-term debt is added to shareholders' equity. This is a significantly different formula than ROIC, however; in comparing ROIC between companies, make sure that the same definition of "total capital" is being employed.

---

### Key Point

Total capital and total capitalization are vastly different values. Be sure you know which one is being used to calculate return on invested capital.

---

The third combined ratio is called *return on assets (ROA)*. This is a comparison between net return and total assets. Several variations of this are used, adjusting both sides of the equation, so—as is the case with all ratios compared between different companies—make sure the information employed is uniform in each case.

ROA is calculated by dividing the period's return by the ending value of assets:

$$\text{net return} \div \text{total assets} = \text{ROA}$$

The net return may be adjusted to add back the interest expense for the year, on the theory that interest is a nonoperating expense, especially when it is related to repayments of bonds and other long-term debts. It is also possible to remove intangible assets from the equation so that net return is compared only to tangible assets; the greater the dollar value of intangibles, the greater difference this makes. However, if long-term debt is exceptionally high and was used to invest in capital assets, this may also distort the calculation. For this reason, a comparison between net return and equity is a more reliable test.

| **Key Point** |
| --- |
| Return on total assets is flawed; when long-term debt is high and proceeds were used to buy capital assets, the calculation is misleading. Comparing net return to equity is much more reliable. |

The many forms of combined ratios demonstrate that there is value in combining indicators. This applies to fundamental and technical comparisons like P/E, as well as to ratios comparing income statement to balance sheet values.

- *The historical value of fundamentals gains context when compared with the current price-based trend.* The fundamental record of a company is most valuable when studied as part of a long-term trend. However, it is historical and thus limited, because by today's standard, the entire financial record of a company may be out of date. This is especially true when the mix of segments and markets has changed since the latest reported year. For this reason, fundamentals can be validated to a degree by incorporating changes in technical indicators to identify emerging new trends. If a technical trend (such as increased volatility) is a symptom of changing fundamental status of the company, this merging of both types of indicators makes sense. Using indicators such as trading range breadth and how it changes, breakouts from established trading range, and emerging new price levels (not to mention changing P/E) can all serve as early signals of changing fundamentals as well.

A technical analyst also makes a mistake by ignoring fundamentals. The historical record may be outdated by the day's ever-changing price trends, but you will discover that the predictability of year-to-year results directly affects price volatility. Technical analysts can make good use of fundamentals in many of the same ways as fundamentals analysts use technical signals. These include:

- *Exceptional changes in the fundamentals signal emerging changes in price and in price volatility.* Traders, like investors, can easily recognize the relationship between fundamental reliability over many years and levels of volatility in the stock price. The more reliable and consistent the fundamentals, the more predictable the price trend within the short term. However, the real value of tracking fundamentals comes when those long-term indicators and trends begin to change. This occurs in both ways. A previously weak set of indicators may gradually develop into a stronger and more consistent record; or a previously consistent set of indicators may begin to fall apart. When either of these fundamental changes is underway, you will eventually see a corresponding change in price volatility as well. And the direction of fundamental trend shift may also anticipate a change in the price trend direction.

---

### Key Point

Changes in fundamental trends, even subtle ones, are eventually going to affect technical trends as well. So the fundamentals can provide early clues about coming trend reversals.

---

- *Perception of value and volatility are found in changes in price, but often begin with earnings reports and other fundamental indicators.* It is a mistake for technical analysts to ignore the fundamentals. It is easy to dismiss them as outdated or not directly applicable to price trends. Technicians tend to prefer tracking the interaction between buyers and sellers to spot momentum and volatility. However, your current perception of a stock's value is likely to begin with the earnings report, and to follow up with other fundamental indicators. The earnings report is the key to fundamental trends; however, it also leads the technical trend as well.

---

### Key Point

Even the most dedicated technician can learn a lot about volatility by starting with the earnings report issued each quarter.

---

- *Neither technical nor fundamental indicators develop independently; they are connected to one another although separated by time.* You may find yourself resisting the idea that technical and fundamental analysis can work together. However, this is unavoidable because they are connected. Thinking that the two schools of thought are separate and distinct is a mistake. They are simply different symptoms of the same trend. The focus on the company and the stock separate the two, but that does not mean they are not related. They confirm one another and, more to the point, changes in the strength of the fundamentals often are the first signal of changes in the technical trend as well.

### Key Point

It may surprise some to learn that fundamental and technical trends are directly related. But they are, and the more you study both the more you see the connection.

## The Dividend Timing Trading Strategy

One method for combining technical and fundamental is a trading system based on the timing of a stock's ex-dividend date. This maximizes your return on capital through dividend yield, while also allowing you to move in and out of positions.

The ex-dividend date (also called the *record date*) is the day that stockholders earn dividends. Anyone owning stock before the preannounced ex-dividend date gets the dividend, although actual payment does not occur until several weeks later. Anyone who buys stock after that date does not earn the dividend.

When the ex-dividend date arrives, the value of stock is likely to drop to reflect the value of dividends to be paid out. So if you buy stock timed to show you as the recorded owner as of the ex-dividend date, you will get the dividend but your shares will be reduced in value.

**record date**
the date on which recorded owners of stock earn a declared dividend even though payment does not take place until several weeks after; also called ex-dividend date.

### Key Point

The stock price will fall on ex-dividend date, so the key to this strategy is to pick exceptionally strong companies so the stock price will rebound sooner rather than later.

A strategy involving timing of purchases like this is clearly a trading strategy. The idea is to get in so that you earn the dividend, and then to get out as quickly as possible. Because the value will drop on or right before that date, you need to alter the strategy with a few trading rules:

- *Limit the activity to the strongest companies only.* A trading strategy like this should not be tried on a highly volatile stock, because it relies on the likelihood that the price will rebound quickly after the ex-date decline. A strong demand for shares will be likely to replace the decline in price by a fast recovery; the decline will not be substantial because it merely offsets the dividend, but the strategy relies on strong demand for shares.

- *Be willing to hold shares until price rebounds.* You might need to hold onto shares for some period of time until the price rebounds from the drop on ex-date. In theory, the dividend effect will be completely recovered on the date the dividend is actually paid. Without other influences on the stock price, the ex-date decline should be matched by the value of dividends paid. In reality, though, many other influences are in play. You need to be able and willing to hold shares until the price comes back, because the timing is not going to be certain. Some stocks may take weeks; others will come back the next day or even on the ex-date.

- *Reinvest dividends in partial shares.* You have the choice when you buy shares to take dividends in cash or to reinvest them by purchasing additional partial shares. The reinvestment choice makes sense because (a) it creates a compound return in the dividend, and (b) you may move in and out of the same stock on each quarter's ex-date, so accumulating shares adds to your overall portfolio value and dividend income.

- *Offset decline with purchase of a put at the money or closer to it, if practical.* Another choice is to buy a short-term at-the-money put to offset the expected decline in the stock's price. Short-term means the put will expire within a matter of days or weeks. A put will increase in value point for point with a price decline in the stock once it is in the money. For a put, this means the price has to be lower than the strike price of the put. This is explained in more detail in the next chapter. The problem with buying a put is whether you can find one priced cheaply enough. If the put is too expensive, it could completely wipe out your dividend income, making the strategy pointless. This only works if and when you can achieve a marginal profit in the increased value of the put to offset a lower price of stock. If this results in a net loss, that loss needs to be lower than the dividend income.

The dividend-based trading strategy uses timing of a fundamental (dividend) to increase short-term income through a trading system. It can create exceptional gains if you are using the same capital to move in and out of stock ownership positions.

For example, assume that you have $5,000 to invest in 100 shares of three different stocks, all priced about the same and all yielding a 2 percent dividend each year. If you buy 100 shares of stock A before ex-dividend date, then sell at breakeven or a small profit within one month, the funds are freed up to repeat the trade in stock B, whose ex-dividend date comes in the second month. The same steps are repeated to move into stock C in the third month. Three stocks could be exchanged in this manner for the full year, maximizing dividend yield.

In this simplified example, you turn a 2 percent annual yield into a much higher annual yield by timing your moves. The quarterly dividend, 0.5 percent, is earned *every month* by moving money in and out of stock. That quadruples the annual dividend income to 8 percent instead of 2 percent.

Is this improvement worth the risk? To a conservative investor focused on fundamentals, it might not be. Such an investor will probably prefer to find a high-quality company as a long-term value investment paying a higher-than-average dividend and simply hold onto shares for the long term. However, a trader who is willing to take greater market risks will find this timing strategy very attractive and will be more willing to pursue it.

As with any trading strategy, the companies used to time dividends in this manner must be strong enough to rebound in price after the expected decline on ex-dividend date. The strategy works only if the best stocks are used for the strategy. Many high-quality companies yield an exceptional dividend, making this approach reasonable. The following chart provides an example of three companies for which this strategy could be employed. This is not a recommendation to invest in these companies, but only a means for showing how the strategy works.

| Dividend timing strategy | | | |
|---|---|---|---|
| Company and Symbol | Dividend Yield | Ex-Dividend Cycle | Payment Cycle |
| AT&T (T) | 7.0% | Jan-Apr-Jul-Oct | Feb-May-Aug-Nov |
| Pitney Bowes (PBI) | 6.6% | Feb-May-Aug-Nov | Mar-Jun-Sep-Dec |
| Altria (MO) | 7.0% | Mar-Jun-Sep-Dec | Apr-Jul-Oct-Jan |

This strategy yields an average of 6.9 percent. However, actual annual yield, based on holding each stop for 30 days, would yield:

| |
| --- |
| AT@T quarterly rate 1.75% |
| Pitney Bowes quarterly rate 1.65% |
| Altria quarterly rate 1.75% |
| average = 1.72% |
| 12 months = 20.6% |

Assuming that these positions could be entered and then exited profitably within one month, with each stock held for one month four times during the year, the total dividend yield would be 20.6 percent. This is impressive, assuming it worked out and not accounting for market changes during the year. This also does not account for potential capital gains or losses in each of the positions.

### Key Point

The double-digit return from dividend timing can be even greater when you add in capital gains on the stock—or entirely wiped out when you experience net losses.

Because the changing value of the stock is itself an additional determining factor in whether this strategy works, it makes sense to employ this strategy in companies with exceptionally strong fundamentals; and only in periods when you expect an overall bull market. The strategy relies on the stock holding its value at the very least. Any increases in value add to the impressive dividend yield, but by the same argument any decline in the stock price can easily convert this into a trading loss.

If this strategy is compared to simply holding shares of all three companies, the market risk is identical, but the dividend yield is four times greater. However, the strategy is not for everyone. Traders will find it interesting, but it makes sense only if companies involved are first qualified in terms of fundamental strength and technical volatility.

## Applying the Combined Approach as a Diversification Method

Another aspect in combining analytical approaches is the resulting diversification this method provides. With fundamental analysis, you invariably end up diversifying by the attributes of competitive position or of dividend yield, or simply between different sectors and industries. With the technical approach, diversification is usually accomplished by degrees of market risk (price volatility).

**Key Point**

Beyond expanding your analytical field, using both fundamental and technical indicators enables you to fine-tune your portfolio's diversification.

By combining the two methods, diversification is fine-tuned and can be managed on a higher level. Examples of multianalytical diversification may include:

- Combinations of working capital analysis via current and debt ratios, with narrowing trading range
- Between an improving trend in revenue and profits, along with strengthening uptrend and mid-range P/E ratio
- Higher-than-expected earnings timed with an ending downtrend tracking with a trend line and candlestick formations

These are only examples, but they demonstrate how your methods for (a) picking companies and (b) timing entry and exit can work hand in hand to improve overall profitability.

Another twist on this method is to combine a conservative fundamental strategy (picking solid large-cap companies or a conservative mutual fund, for example) with a higher-risk technical timing strategy. This technical side may be operated on stocks you also own in your portfolio, or on a different grouping of stocks, selected with greater market volatility. In this instance, you recognize the need for a conservative buy-and-hold segment of the fundamentally based portfolio, while also seeking maximum current income on the technical side.

The combined analytical approach may also lead you to a decision to revert from one approach to the other. For example, if you originally picked a company as a value investment but the fundamentals have since changed, the obvious step from a conservative point of view would be to sell shares and move funds elsewhere. However, what do you do if the current trend is continuing to move prices upward?

**Key Point**

Nothing lasts forever. A conservative value company may deteriorate and become a high-risk one. This doesn't mean you have to sell; it could mean the stock is an excellent choice for swing trading.

In this case, you may decide to revert from fundamental to technical and change the buy-and-hold strategy on this company to a swing-trading strategy instead. To protect paper profits, use options (covered calls or long puts) to offset any price decline. Also begin tracking the daily chart to look for signs of a coming reversal through momentum indicators, moving averages, and candlestick patterns.

The point in keeping an open mind to both forms of analysis is that it improves your overall analytical insights. Neither technical nor fundamental analysis provides you with all of the answers you need, but using elements of both is quite helpful. Whether you see the strategy as a form of diversification, confirmation, or a change based on new and emerging trends, the combined analytical approach helps you to improve your interpretation of long-term values and short-term trends, and improves your timing in both strategies.

The kinds of flexible analysis you can accomplish with combined analysis are made even more powerful when you introduce options into the equation. Options are not only speculative, high-risk, complicated tools best used by experts. There are many strategies, some highly conservative and well suited to reducing your market risk. The next chapter introduces options basics and describes a few of the strategies designed to help you manage your portfolio and either increase current income or cut down on risk.

# Chapter 13

# Options to Leverage and Manage Your Portfolio

**M**ost investors and traders start out with two assumptions. First, their stock market activities are going to involve buying and selling shares of stock (either directly or through a mutual fund). Second, the sequence of trades is buy-hold-sell.

Both of these assumptions can be challenged and the stock market universe expanded by also taking a look at the option as an alternative. This may work purely for speculation or as a highly conservative strategy, and can even be used to protect your portfolio from loss.

The advantage in using options is that they can be designed to suit any risk level and any market strategy. Most people have heard that options are complicated and high-risk, but that is only true for some advanced strategies.

---

### Key Point

Options are quite flexible so they can be designed to suit any situation and any risk tolerance level.

---

The two beginning assumptions about entering the market can be expanded to the point of view that there is much more than simply buying and selling stock, and options open up a world of new possibilities. Options also provide a means for going short without the high risks of selling stock short. In a short position, the sequence of trades is sell-hold-buy (or with options,

**call**
an option providing its owner the right—but not the obligation—to buy 100 shares of a specified stock, at a fixed price, on or before a specified expiration date.

**put**
an option providing its owner the right—but not the obligation—to sell 100 shares of a specified stock, at a fixed price, on or before a specified expiration date.

**strike**
the fixed price of an option, at which the owner is allowed to trade 100 shares of stock.

it is also possible to have the sequence sell-hold-expire). Using options is not always a high-risk approach; it can be designed to be exceptionally conservative.

# Definitions and Basics

There are two kinds of options, both traded publicly on the open exchanges. First is the *call*, which is an intangible contract giving its owner the right, but not the obligation, to buy 100 shares of stock at a fixed price. Second is the *put*, which is the opposite. The put gives its owner the right, but not the obligation, to *sell* 100 shares of stock at a fixed price.

Every option has a specific and fixed price called the *strike*. This is the price at which the owner of a call is allowed to buy 100 shares even if the current market price is much higher; or the price at which the owner of a put is allowed to sell 100 shares even if the current market price is much lower.

In addition to a fixed and unchanging strike price, every option is also tied to a specific *expiration date*. That is the date when the option will become worthless. It is the Saturday immediately after the third Friday of the specified expiration month.

The final unchanging attribute of every option is the *underlying security* on which it is traded. This can be a stock, an ETF, or a commodity. Most people starting out in the market are likely to begin with options on stock. The underlying security is fixed and cannot be transferred or replaced.

Collectively, these attributes of options—type of option (call or put), strike, expiration date, and underlying security—are referred to as an option's *terms*. These terms are fixed and unchanging, and while many options are likely to be available at any time, each one is defined by the terms.

**Key Point**

Every option's terms are fixed and cannot be changed; this ensures an orderly market for trading in option contracts.

There are several possible outcomes for both buyers and sellers of options. In each case, you can buy an option that grants you the rights spelled out by the terms. If you sell an option, you give up those rights, meaning someone else could *exercise* the option. If you sell a call and it is exercised, 100 shares of the underlying stock are called away and you are required to deliver those shares at the strike price. If you sell a put and it is exercised, 100 shares of the underlying stock are put to you at the strike price.

A seller of either option faces the risk of exercise. A call will be exercised only when the current price per share is higher than the strike; and a put will be exercised only when the current price per share is lower than the strike. For the owner of either option, the strike is fixed so an advantage to exercise is in the ability to buy 100 shares below current value (exercising a call), or to sell 100 shares above current value (exercising a put).

**expiration date**
the date when an option becomes worthless; the Saturday following the third Friday of the specified expiration month.

**underlying security**
the stock or other security controlled by the option. In the case of options on stock, every option contract controls 100 shares of the underlying security.

## Valuation of Options

The option's value is called its *premium*. This is the current value of each option contract. It is expressed as a single numeral with two decimal places. For example, an option might be priced currently at 2.40. This means it is worth $240.

Value contains three distinct and separate parts, making valuation of options more complex than that of stock. With stock, the current market value is widely understood as the price per share. With options, the premium is broken out into components based on the proximity between strike and current value of the underlying stock, time to expiration, and volatility of the underlying stock.

**terms**
the four attributes of every option that cannot be changed or replaced: type of option (call or put), strike, expiration date, and underlying security.

### Key Point

Option valuation consists of three different segments, which vary based on proximity between strike and stock price, and by time and stock volatility.

**exercise**
the act by an owner of a call to buy shares at the fixed strike price, or by the owner of a put to sell shares at the fixed strike price.

**premium**
the value of an option. This is expressed as a numeral without dollar signs and with two decimal places, denoting the value per share. A premium of 2.40, for example, means the option is priced at $240.

**intrinsic value**
the portion of an option's premium when the current value of stock is higher than the call's strike or lower than the put's strike.

The first value is called *intrinsic value*. This is the value equal to the number of points that the stock is above a call's strike or below a put's strike. For example, a 35 call has intrinsic value of three points ($300) when the stock is worth $38 per share; and a 45 put has intrinsic value of two points ($200) when the stock is worth $43.

Intrinsic value can only exist when the current value of stock is greater than the call's strike or less than the put's strike. In this condition, the option is described as *in the money*.

In comparison, no intrinsic value exists when the current value of stock is at or below the call's strike, or when the stock's value is at or above the put's strike. When the value and strike are equal, the option is *at the money* and when the value is lower than the call's strike or higher than the put's strike, the option is *out of the money*.

The second of three components making up the option's overall premium value is called *time value*. This is the value assigned solely to the amount of time remaining until expiration. The longer the time remaining in the life of an option, the higher the time value will be. The rate of decline is very slow when options have a long time remaining; as expiration approaches, the time decay of the option accelerates. The rate of decline is faster, so the total history of time value looks much like a 30-year amortization chart; the principal balance falls gradually and then picks up speed in the final years. For options, the same path is seen in the decline of time value.

### Key Point

Time value is very predictable and can be tracked based on expiration, with the decline in time value accelerating in the last two months.

The third and final type of option premium is the volatility value, usually described as implied volatility of the option. This is also called *extrinsic value*. Whereas both intrinsic and time value are entirely predictable, extrinsic value is where all of the unknown changes take place, based on volatility of the underlying stock and proximity between current value and strike of the option.

Extrinsic value often offsets changes in intrinsic value, resulting in less price reaction to movement in the underlying stock. For example, when in the money an option moves only two points while the stock's price moves three points. The one-point difference reflects a change in extrinsic value.

The option premium is complex when you realize that it contains three distinct parts. However, both intrinsic value and time value are easily understood and completely predictable. So all variables in option valuation are involved with extrinsic value. The factors affecting implied volatility found in extrinsic value include:

**in the money**
the status of an option when current value is higher than the call's strike or lower than the put's strike.

- Time to expiration, with a tendency for extrinsic value to offset changes in intrinsic value to a greater degree when more time is involved.

- Proximity between current value of stock and strike of the option, so that when option strikes are deep in the money (more than five points), value is less likely to move point for point with changes in the stock because extrinsic value is more likely to offset intrinsic value.

**at the money**
the status of an option when its strike is equal to the current value of the underlying stock.

- Time and proximity in conjunction; as expiration nears and as the current value moves closer to a strike, extrinsic value is likely to become less influential on price movement.

- Changes in volatility of the underlying stock, so that if the stock's breadth of trading expands or if a price breakout occurs and a strong uptrend or downtrend follows, the greater stock volatility causes greater option volatility, as extrinsic value has strong influence on overall option premium.

**out of the money**
the status of an option when current value is lower than the call's strike or higher than the put's strike.

The premium is complex and changes are likely to be subtle, even when price movement (notably in the money) is obvious. Valuation of options combines known values (intrinsic and time value) with the great unknown influences on the stock's price.

**Key Point**

Valuation of options is based on time and proximity between strike and current price, as well as on overall stock volatility.

**time value**
the portion of an option's premium that varies with time remaining to expiration; the farther away the expiration date, the higher the time value. This value declines gradually until the last two months, when time value falls rapidly, ending at zero on expiration day.

**extrinsic value**
the portion of an option's premium beyond both intrinsic value and time value, reflecting the implied volatility of the option and varying based on time to expiration and proximity between current value of stock and strike price of the option. The price volatility of the underlying stock also directly impacts the extrinsic value of the option.

To better understand how extrinsic value works, imagine this situation: A call's strike is 7 points above current value of the stock, meaning it is deep out of the money. The option expires in nine months. The combination of the extended life and the proximity make this a very cheap option. However, within the next month, the stock rises by nine points, so the option is two points in the money. The overall value of the option in terms of intrinsic and extrinsic value increases; intrinsic value moves from zero to two points, but the overall value of the option has risen by five points.

This is a puzzling situation until the relationship between pricing and volatility is understood. In this case, time value has declined slightly because expiration is one month closer. Intrinsic value is equal to the points in the money. However, the difference between 7 points out and 2 points in is significant. It is not only the 9-point change that matters, but the change in status. Now the option is in the money but still has eight months until expiration. Its extrinsic value is much greater now because the opportunities for further intrinsic changes have increased greatly due to the movement in the underlying stock.

To complicate matters even more, this example is only hypothetical. There is no predictability in how extrinsic value will change based on dramatic movement in the underlying stock. There are only tendencies and likely extrinsic adjustments, but you also have to remember that volatility is an uncertain matter in pricing of all markets. Making a distinction between the three types of valuation clarifies some of the mysteries of option pricing, but uncertainty—even when an option is in the money—is still the ruling attribute of the overall premium level.

## Basic Long Option Strategies

The rudiments of options are not easy to grasp, and for that reason trying some paper trading makes sense. This helps you to try out basic strategies, master terminology, and learn how the system works.

However, paper trading is safe because no money is actually at risk, so its value is limited to the *concept* of options trading and not to its real-world application.

| **Key Point** |
| --- |
| Paper trading is a good way to learn the rules of options trading, but that value is limited because no real money is at risk. |

In addition, your brokerage firm will not allow you to just jump in and trade advanced options. You have to complete an options trading application in which you tell your brokerage firm how much experience and knowledge you possess. Based on what you say and on the value of your portfolio, you will then be assigned a "trading level" you will be allowed to pursue.

At first you will be allowed only to execute the most basic options strategies. The first step for options trading is the long position. Buying calls or puts gives you experience and exposure to the benefits and risks of options. A single option contract allows you to control 100 shares of the underlying stock, but you are not obligated to exercise the option. You can sell at any time you want, either to take a profit or to cut losses.

When you buy a call, you expect to make a profit if the stock's market value rises. However, it has to rise far enough and fast enough to move higher than the premium you pay to buy the call. Because time value is decaying as expiration approaches, you will need to have a substantial point gain in the underlying stock if the call will rise far enough and fast enough.

When you buy a put, you will earn a profit if the underlying stock's value declines. The lower the value falls, the more valuable the put will become. As with calls, the time value of puts has to be offset.

| **Key Point** |
| --- |
| Option buyers have to struggle with the balance between time and premium; the longer the time, the higher the premium and the more difficult it becomes to overcome that cost to create a profit. |

For both types of options, time is the enemy. For example, if you buy an option that is at the money (meaning the strike is identical to the current market value per share of the underlying stock) and you pay 4 ($400), a price rise of four points in the money only leads to a breakeven (before deducting trading expenses). Four points of intrinsic value only covers your initial cost of the option. So you need *more* than the cost of the option in order to make a profit.

For this reason, about three out of every four options expires worthless or is closed at a loss. In other words, trading long options is risky.

The dilemma for every trader is picking the best option. To get price movement, you need to pick options close to current value of the stock, but ideally right at or just removed from the money. So the ideal call is going to have a strike one to two points higher than current market value, and the ideal put is going to have a strike at the money or one to two points lower than the underlying stock's current value.

With the proximity between strike and stock value as close as possible, you have the best chance of experiencing price growth adequate to cover and exceed your cost. However, there are two problems you have to deal with, and picking the best option is a balancing act.

The first problem involves *cost*. The proximity of strike to value of the stock affects the premium level. You can buy deep out of the money options very cheaply, but the chances of making a profit are more remote because the stock's price must move substantially before expiration. So the closer your option is to current value, the more it is going to cost, even when out-of-the-money. The changes in price between one point and six points between strike and current value are caused by extrinsic value.

The second problem is *time*. The closer the option to expiration, the cheaper it is because time value and extrinsic value will be minimal. However, time value is also going to be declining at the fastest rate in the last two months of the option's life span. So a "cheap" option that is cheap because it will soon expire is also a long shot. So you probably need to buy an option with some time remaining before expiration. However, the further away expiration is, the more expensive the option. This is due to time value; in addition, a long time to expiration also means that extrinsic value may work as an offset; so if the option moves in the money, the overall value may not move point for point with intrinsic value. Extrinsic value may make overall premium less responsive, adding to the problem. Not only did you pay more for the option, but even in the money its value is not growing as fast as you would like.

**Key Point**

Options close to expiration are cheap. However, they have only limited time for profits to develop, and time value declines rapidly as expiration nears.

The basic long strategies are a challenge because it is so difficult to profit with them. You fight time and cost and need to look for bargain prices for the time period you want to have available for your option.

The uses of long strategies are varied. These include:

- *Pure speculation.* You can buy calls or puts simply to speculate in the market. The leverage is significant, because for relatively small amounts of capital you control 100 shares of stock. This makes speculating in options very appealing, but remember, most long options do not end up profitably.

- *Swing trading and timing.* Options are used effectively for swing trading in place of stock. You can use long calls at the bottom and long puts at the top of identified short-term swings, reducing the swing-trading risks, enabling you to leverage capital, and avoiding the problems of needing to short shares of stock at topside reversals.

- *Insurance for paper profits.* You can buy puts when your stock value has risen substantially to insure profits. In this situation, you face a dilemma: You expect the stock price to reverse and decline to a degree because it has risen too quickly, but you do not want to sell shares. In this situation, buying puts insures your profits. If the stock continues to rise, you are out the put premium; if the stock price falls, the put increases in value and offsets the stock loss. The put can then be closed at a profit or exercised so you can sell shares at a strike above current market value.

- *Parts of more complex strategies.* The long option also plays a key role in strategies involving offsetting positions (long versus short or call versus put, for example), of which there are dozens of possible combinations. In other words, long options are not always separate and distinct as strategies, but also act as parts of more complex strategies.

The long option is high-risk in the sense that three out of four instances will lose, on average; but in terms of capital risk, it is a low-risk approach, because you can never lose more than the premium you pay to open the long option. This is a 100 percent loss, of course; but it is a relatively small dollar amount when compared to the market risk of buying 100 shares.

**covered call**
a short call opened when the trader also owns 100 shares of the underlying stock. In the event of exercise, the shares are called away at the strike.

# Covered Calls

Another basic strategy is the *covered call*, which is a two-part strategy. First you must own 100 shares of the underlying stock. Then a call is sold and the risks of going short are covered by the shares. In the event of exercise, your 100 shares are called away at the strike. As long as the strike is picked at a level higher than your original cost for those shares, the exercise is profitable in three ways. You keep the option premium, you continue to earn dividends while you hold the shares, and you have a capital gain upon exercise of the call.

Just as time is the enemy of a buyer, it is the friend of a seller. Declining time value means more profits for sellers, making covered calls more likely to turn out profitably than buying options.

---

### Key Point

Time works against buyers, making long option strategies difficult to execute profitably. However, for covered call selling, the same attribute works in the seller's favor, making covered calls far more profitable in most cases.

---

There are two possible outcomes from the covered call:

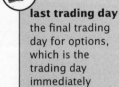

**last trading day**
the final trading day for options, which is the trading day immediately before the third Saturday of the expiration month.

1. *The stock rises above strike.* If the stock price is higher than the strike at the point of expiration, the call will be exercised and your 100 shares of stock will be called away at the strike price. With this in mind, the strike you pick for a covered call should always be higher than the price per share you paid to buy the stock. Also remember that a short call can be exercised at any time. The most likely time is the *last trading day*, which is the trading day (usually Friday unless a holiday) right before the third Saturday of expiration month. Calls might also be exercised on ex-dividend date or at any other time that the call is in the money. Your overall profit consists of the call premium, dividends earned, and capital gains on the stock.

You can also avoid exercise with the *rolling strategy*. This involves closing the short call and replacing it with another call that expires later. This produces more net income because more time equals more premium. It also delays exercise in most cases. If you can roll forward and up to a higher strike, this further reduces exercise risk, or, if the short call is exercised later, a higher capital gain is earned.

2. *The stock price falls below strike.* As long as the stock price remains at or below strike of the short call, that call will not be exercised. You can wait out expiration, after which the call becomes worthless and

the premium is 100 percent profit; or you can close out a call and take a short-term profit on the net difference between the original sale and the closing purchase prices. You can open and then close covered calls as often as you wish.

**rolling strategy**
closing a short option and replacing it with another option that expires later, with the intention of deferring or avoiding exercise.

Covered call writing is a conservative strategy because the market risk is lower than the market risk of just owning shares. This is true because the premium you earn from selling the call discounts your net basis in the stock. As long as the strike is higher than the original price per share you paid for the stock, your profit from covered calls that are exercised has three parts: call premium, dividends, and capital gains on the stock. When a call expires or is closed at a profit, you are free to repeat the strategy as many times as you wish.

**uncovered call**
a short call written when the trader does not also own 100 shares of the underlying stock; a high-risk option strategy.

### Key Point

The risks to covered call writing are fairly low when compared to simply owning shares, because the premium income discounts the stock's basis.

There are three primary risks to writing covered calls:

**naked call**
alternate name for an uncovered call.

- Your money is tied up for as long as the covered call remains open. You cannot sell shares without exposing the call by converting it to an *uncovered call* (also called a *naked call*). While the covered call is low-risk, the uncovered call is very high-risk because in the event of exercise, you would need to make up the difference between strike price and market value of the stock. The other alternative to free up capital is to close the short call, which is not always desirable.

**writer**
a trader who opens, or writes, a short position in options.

- The call may be exercised. If you open a covered call, you have to be willing to accept exercise and have your 100 shares called away. If you are not willing to give up shares, a covered call is not an appropriate strategy.

**spreads**
option strategies combining two or more options on the same underlying stock, but with different strikes, or different expiration dates, or both.

- Opportunity for further capital gains is lost. If a covered call is exercised, it means the stock's price moved above the call's strike. No matter how high the price has moved, you are required to deliver your 100 shares at the strike price. A covered call *writer* has to be completely willing to give up the possible higher appreciation on shares of stock in exchange for the certainty of the call premium.

## The Flexibility of Options

**vertical spreads**
spreads opened with options on the same underlying stock with identical expiration dates but different strike prices.

Options have dozens of uses beyond the basic strategies. They can be used to open *spreads*, for example. These are strategies consisting of opening two or more different options at the same time and on the same underlying stock, but with different strikes, or different expiration dates, or both.

> **Key Point**
>
> Spreads can be designed with varying levels of risk based on perceptions about the direction stock prices are most likely to move.

There are three different ways to create a spread. The first refers to different strike prices (*vertical spreads*). These are spreads opened on the same expiration month but with different strikes.

The second type is the opposite, with options at the same strike price but different expiration months (*horizontal spreads*), also called *calendar spreads*).

The third type of spread has different strike prices *and* expiration dates (*diagonal spreads*). These are a combination of the vertical and horizontal spreads.

**horizontal spreads**
spreads opened with options on the same underlying stock with identical strike prices but different expiration months.

Spreads come in a great variety of forms involving only calls, only puts, or both; and consisting of long positions only, short positions only, or both long and short positions. The construction of the spread defines its level of risk as well as the maximum and minimum levels of profit or loss that can be earned at given price levels.

> ### Key Point
>
> Spreads can be constructed using calls only, puts only, long positions, short positions, and combinations of both. They are among the most flexible of option strategies.

**calendar spreads**
alternative name for horizontal spreads.

Another expanded form of options is a series of strategies known as *straddles*. These consist of opening call or put positions with identical strike prices and expiration dates. They may be long or short. Long straddles require paying out cash in the hope that one side or the other (call or put) with gain enough value to surpass the cost of the straddle. A short straddle produces income but involves greater risks as well.

Straddles, like spreads, can be quite complex and involved in their construction. They are designed to create limited profit or loss ranges in price, based on the trader's belief about the most likely direction of price movement in the underlying stock.

**diagonal spreads**
spreads opened with options on the same underlying stock with different strike prices and different expiration months.

> ### Key Point
>
> Straddles invariably involve a limited profit potential, limited loss potential, or both.

**straddles**
option strategies involving opening of call and put positions with the same strike and expiration.

A final use of options is the creation of a *synthetic position*. This is a combination of options that mirror the price changes in other positions, such as stock. For example, a synthetic stock position will change by growing by one point when the underlying stock price rises, or falling by one point when the underlying stock price falls.

Options are flexible tools that can be used in many different ways and at different risk levels. The danger to a novice trader is in entering option positions without fully understanding the risk that is involved. With experience, traders learn that options can provide many levels of usefulness from speculation to advanced portfolio management.

The next chapter proposes a method for taking ideas from both investing and trading strategies to build a sensible approach to the stock market that works best for you based on experience, resources, and risk tolerance.

**synthetic position**
an option position involving two or more open contracts designed to act in the same manner as another security, such as stock.

# Your Sensible Approach
# to the Market

Whether you decide to approach the stock market as an investor or as a trader, or by combining both disciplines, your success is going to rely on how effectively you gain experience and knowledge and put your resources to work.

Resources include your income and investment cash levels. Of course, the more money you have to place into investments and trades, the more market exposure you can gain. However, that will not always mean that your portfolio will outperform smaller ones. The exposure to profitable opportunities is always accompanied by an equally important exposure to possible losses.

The key to market success is found in improving not only your analytical skills, but also your timing. Entry and exit timing can never be perfect, but when you discover how to analyze both fundamental and technical indicators with skill, you will improve your rate of success.

## Popular Stock Market Myths

The stock market is a culture based partly on persistent myths. To a large extent, belief in myths is wishful thinking and, in some cases, magical thinking. This is a belief in something that simply does not make sense. For example, if you believe that watching a baseball game while wearing the team hat or a "lucky" shirt leads to victory, this is magical thinking.

| **Key Point** |
| --- |
| The stock market has many myths, and a large number of investors and traders believe them, even though they are not true. |

Magical thinking is quite common. It is an attempt to find a correlation between acts (wearing a lucky shirt, for example) or rituals (sitting in a lucky chair) and outcomes (a win for your team or profit in your stock). The other side of superstition in magical thinking is the fear that saying a particular thing or doing something causes bad luck or a bad outcome. Actors claim that saying "good luck" to someone is actually bad luck, preferring "break a leg" as an opposite form of good wishes. Actors also believe they should never whistle backstage or say "Macbeth." These are forms of acts or utterances that are believed to bring about a bad outcome. In the stock market, many investors and traders hold similar beliefs even though they are not always entirely aware of them. Belief in odd timing systems is one example. Some believe that outcomes of the Super Bowl, weather patterns, or even the width of tree rings determine stock market performance—rather than economic trends and the influence of supply and demand.

In the volatile and fast-moving modern stock market, techniques of trading, breadth of markets, costs of trading, and availability of research have all made everything much faster, more efficient, and immediate. However, some popular myths persist. These include:

- *The entry price of an investment is always the "zero" point.* Many investors and traders operate on the flawed assumption that their entry price is "zero," meaning that from that point, prices are going to rise. This might happen, but prices might also fall. It is important to realize that today's price is part of a never-changing struggle between buyers and sellers, and no trend lasts forever.

- *Buying high-value stocks and then forgetting about them is a wise method.* Some value investors advise that conservative investors should not look at the daily stock market news or spend too much time worrying about the price of their stocks. Some have even advised not reviewing the market at all after a good purchase has been made. But there is a balance. The fortunes of today's "good" companies can change and if and when that happens, even the most conservative buy-and-hold investor will want to get out and replace that company with one that better meets their standards. You might not want to review the market every day, but you do need to monitor what you own periodically to make sure yesterday's positive indicators still hold.

Even buy-and-hold strategies require a degree of monitoring to ensure that companies continue to meet the fundamental standards to be kept in the portfolio.

---

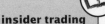

- *Past mistakes should be studied, analyzed, and revisited in order to improve future performance and avoid the same mistakes.* There is a lot to be learned from past mistakes. But many investors and traders find themselves dwelling on their miscues and allowing these errors to affect how they operate today. It is a mistake, for example, to avoid a strategy only because it did not work in the past; it makes more sense to learn from mistakes to help avoid repeating them. Another mistake is to try to earn a larger profit on today's trade to make up for the loss on yesterday's trade. Increasing risks in this manner is not advisable. Always stay with your risk profile. Accept losses. And move forward, not back.

**insider trading**
the act of trading in the market based on information not available to the general public and provided by a source inside an organization or in a position to know news the general public does not have.

- *Inside tips give you an edge on everyone else.* The persistent belief in the insider tip characterizes a lot of the stock market culture. Two things should be kept in mind, however. First, stock tips are not reliable as a reason to put money in today. Second, a true inside tip from someone with knowledge not available to everyone else is not supposed to be shared. It is illegal to accept and act on insider information. The federal civil and criminal laws governed by the Securities and Exchange Commission (SEC) regulate *insider trading*. If you get tips from an online chat room, you have no idea who is advising that you buy stocks. Some people buy shares and then promote buying by others to run the price up, so they can sell at a profit. This practice, called *pump and dump*, is also illegal.

**pump and dump**
the purchase of shares and encouragement of others to do the same, hoping to drive prices higher and then sell at a profit.

- *The institutional traders are experts, and individuals cannot compete with them.* Big institutional investors (mutual funds, pension plans, insurance companies, for example) may have portfolios in the billions of dollars and hire a team of full-time professional researchers and experts. Ironically, this does not guarantee better-than-average performance, in spite of the myth claiming this. The truth is that most mutual funds perform *below* market averages:

Because of their excessive annual fees and poor execution, approximately 80% of mutual funds underperform the stock market's returns in a typical year. Over the past couple of years, that number has been going up, as mutual funds have been raising their fees to even higher levels. The average actively managed stock mutual fund returns approximately 2% less per year to its shareholders than the stock market returns in general.[1]

- *Diversification is not a smart way to invest; find a great stock and put all your money into it.* A reckless idea is to put all of your money into a single stock, unless you know somehow that the stock's value is going to rise—and of course you cannot know this. Diversifying too broadly does average out your net return, but a moderate level of diversification is just prudent.

### Key Point

Diversification is simply smart management. Putting all of your capital at risk on any one company is a high-risk idea.

- *Successful investors know the secrets to beating the market, but do not always want to share those secrets with others.* The fact is, there are no secret formulas to market success. Successful investors or traders earn profits through diligent research, hard work, and learning from their mistakes. There is no "easy way" to get rich quick.
- *Day trading and swing trading are the ways to make fast profits.* The appeal of a fast turnaround is difficult to resist, but thinking that the day systems are easy and a "sure thing" is a very risky thing to believe. The science of timing and reading of entry and exit signals is complex and requires experience and practice.
- *Theories like the EMT and random walk prove that no one can really beat the markets.* A cynical point of view is that the market is so

---

[1] Bill Barker, *The Performance of Mutual Funds,* at The Motley Fool, www.fool.com.

efficient that you cannot beat the odds, or that price movement is so random that there is no way to know what to buy. Neither of these theories holds up when analyzed over time, and common sense tells you that the beliefs among people with "skin in the game" (money in the market) know much more about it than academic theories claim to know.

- *To understand fundamentals you have to be an accountant, and to understand technicals you need a degree in math.* Some people have concluded that any form of detailed analysis requires credentials. However, the basic fundamental and technical indicators everyone needs to study can be comprehended without any special training or knowledge. It's all a matter of side-by-side comparison, long-term trend observation, and common sense. A good rule to follow is that if something is too complicated to understand, it probably is not a valuable indicator, either.

## Going Forward from Here

How much can you learn simply by studying? You can read books, study information on web sites, attend seminars, and spend months in paper trading. Yet when that is all done, you still do not really understand investing and trading until you put money into a position and find out what happens.

| Key Point |
| --- |
| No matter how much you study and analyze, you cannot understand the market until you have money at risk. |

There are no fast or easy ways to get around the learning curve. In spite of some claims to the contrary, you need to gather information and knowledge as part of the process of learning how markets work. Some suggestions:

- Don't pay for information when exaggerated promises are part of the deal. No seminar is going to provide you with stock market secrets or shortcuts, and no program is going to help you to know at the push of a button which stocks to buy or avoid.
- Make up your own mind and lead; don't follow. Those who follow tend to enter and exit positions after the big move has taken place.
- Consider and use all valid kinds of information. Fundamental investors can gain insight from candlestick charts and moving averages, and

devoted chartists can learn a lot from the latest earnings report or quarterly dividend announcement. Remember, all sources of information about companies and stock prices are part of the same overall market body of knowledge.

- Listen and learn. You can gain more knowledge about markets from other investors and traders than you can from financial reporters on television or radio programs. Get facts from other individual investors, investment clubs, articles, and books, and don't rely on 30-second sound bites.

The process of deciding how and why to invest or trade is a very individual one. It has to be based on your personal risk tolerance, unending analysis and evaluation, and a matching up of appropriate investments and trading strategies. Every case should be done on a comparative basis, between companies, between fiscal years, and between trading periods. The more comparisons you make, the more reliable your overall understanding of how prices move and how companies grow.

# Glossary

**12b-1 fee**  a fee charged by a mutual fund for marketing and promotion to attract new investors.

**accumulated depreciation**  the sum of all years' depreciation expense recorded and claimed. The annual expense is offset by the accumulation account, which is a negative asset, or a reduction of the book value of capital assets.

**accumulation phase**  the first phase of a trend, during which contrarians and experienced investors and traders buy (in an uptrend) or sell (in a downtrend).

**accumulation/distribution line**  an analysis of volume in relation to price, based on the CMF theory and stating that volume trends precede price movement.

**amortization**  the yearly amount of expense recorded and offset by a reduction to a prepaid asset account. For example, when a 36-month insurance premium is prepaid, it is amortized over the 36 months rather than reported as expense in the year paid.

**annual report**  a financial and marketing summary issued by corporations, including financial statements and detailed explanations, and management's interpretation of its financial and competitive position in the market.

**ascending triangle**  a pattern of narrowing breadth in the trading range, consisting of flat resistance and rising support, and preceding a likely reversal and downtrend.

**at the money**  the status of an option when its strike is equal to the current value of the underlying stock.

**back-end sales load**  a variation of sales commission in a mutual fund, in which the commission is deducted when shares are redeemed rather than when investments are made.

**balance sheet**  a financial statement reporting the balances of all asset, liability, and net worthy accounts as of the last day of the reporting period.

**balanced funds**  mutual funds combining growth and income positions based on positions in stocks or combinations of stocks and bonds.

**basket of stocks**  the preidentified, fixed portfolio in the exchange-traded fund (ETF).

**bear markets**  markets of declining price trends over a period of months or years.

**blue chip**  companies with strong earnings, a history of regular dividend payments, and little or no long-term liabilities; a financially strong and stable company.

**book value**  the true value of a company based on balance sheet reporting; it is the total of all assets minus the total of all liabilities. When the net value is divided by outstanding shares, the result is book value per share.

**breadth**   the span of price movement within the current trading range, representing the number of points of movement over time.

**breakaway gap**   a type of gap that moves prices above or below the trading range and either begins a rally or retreats to the previous level in subsequent sessions.

**break-even rate**   the rate of return needed from investing activity to absorb inflation and taxes, in order to maintain the purchasing power of investment capital.

**breakout**   price movement below support or above resistance, signifying creation of a new trading range or a failed attempt in which prices retreat back to the established trading range.

**bull markets**   markets characterized by generally rising prices of stocks over a period of months or years.

**buy and hold**   an investment strategy involving identification of value investments and purchase of shares, with the intention of holding those shares for the long term.

**buy to open/sell to open**   the type of opening order being placed. A buy to open is used to create a long position, and a sell to open creates a short position.

**calendar spreads**   alternative name for horizontal spreads.

**call**   an option providing its owner the right but not the obligation to buy 100 shares of a specified stock, at a fixed price, on or before a specified expiration date.

**candlesticks**   chart entries based on rectangular boxes that show at a glance the opening and closing price, trading range, and direction of price movement for a trading session.

**capital assets**   all assets set up to be periodically depreciated because their value outlasts a single accounting year; when fully depreciated, the capital asset's book value is zero.

**capitalization-based funds**   mutual funds specializing in portfolios of companies based on market capitalization (large-cap, mid-cap, or small-cap).

**capitalization-weighted average**   a stock market average in which components are weighted according to their market capitalization rather than by price per share.

**Chaikin Money Flow (CMF)**   an oscillator that identifies overbought or oversold conditions through a mathematical analysis of price trends.

**channel**   trading within the bounds of resistance and support, which does not break through on either side.

**chartist**   a trader who studies price patterns through a series of stock charts, looking for early signs for emerging entry or exit points based on how price and volume behave, and using a range of possible technical indicators to make those decisions.

**circuit breaker**   an automatic halt to trading in all listed securities on exchanges, triggered by exceptionally large price declines and set to last a specified number of hours or until the end of trading for the session.

**closed-end fund**   a mutual fund with a maximum number of shares outstanding that trades over a stock exchange rather than directly between fund management and investors. Market value of shares rises or falls based on demand and performance rather than on the market value of the portfolio.

**closing order**   an order placed with a broker to close a position, whether it had been opened long or short.

**common gap**   a price gap occurring as a part of normal trading activity and without any signal value for changes in the existing trend.

**common stock**   (called "ordinary shares" in the UK) ownership in a corporation including voting rights for membership on boards of directors and corporate policies. Common stockholders have the lowest priority in the event of liquidation, below bond-holders and preferred stockholders.

**conduit investment**   any organization that passes through profits to its investors and manages a collective portfolio. The best-known conduit investment is the mutual fund.

**confirmation**   the use of one indicator to bolster or support the conclusions reached by what a different indicator reveals.

**congestion**   a price pattern of sideways movement within a narrow trading range, with neither buyers nor sellers in control.

**consolidation**   a period of indecision in the market, during which neither buyers nor sellers are in command. No one can determine whether prices will be driven higher or lower, so there is little or no movement during this time.

**contingent deferred sales load (CDSL)**   a back-end load, or sales commission assessed by mutual funds only if shares are redeemed before a specified number of years.

**continuation day**   a single day with a candlestick pattern providing a sign of a continuation in the trend rather than reversal, due to its position and direction within the trend.

**contrarian**   an investor or trader who makes decisions based on analysis rather than simply following the majority and who recognizes that the majority is wrong more often than right, so making the opposite decision often is the smart move.

**convergence theory**   a theory that crowd behavior is created by individuals who bring ideas to the crowd, rather than as a spontaneous matter. In the market, individuals who act in a particular way may influence others to follow their behavior.

**convergence/divergence**   in technical analysis, the pattern revealed in two moving averages of different numbers of sessions. As the lines move closer together (converge) or farther apart (diverge) the chartist draws conclusions about the coming price direction.

**core earnings**   a calculated adjustment to net earnings to isolate earnings from the company's primary, or core business. All noncore, nonrecurring, or extraordinary items are adjusted out of the calculation of net earnings allowed under the accounting rules.

**cost of goods sold**   expenditures for merchandise, direct labor, freight, and the changes in inventory levels, all attributable directly to generation of revenue.

**covered call**   a short call opened when the trader also owns 100 shares of the underlying stock. In the event of exercise, the shares are called away at the strike.

**current assets**   all assets in liquid form, meaning cash or convertible to cash within 12 months.

**current liabilities**   all debts payable within 12 months, including the current portion of long-term liabilities.

**current ratio**   a popular test of working capital. Current assets are divided by current liabilities, and the answer is expressed as a single digit.

**cycle**   an economic tendency for sales volume and profits to change predictably due to economic or calendar timing. Among the best-known of market cycles is that experienced in the retail trade, which goes through specific seasons of high and low sales volume based on consumer buying habits.

**day trading**   activity in which positions are entered and exited on the same day so that no open positions remain by the end of the day.

**debt ratio**   an indicator derived by dividing long-term debt by total capitalization.

**deferred assets**   expense payments made in one year but belonging completely to a future year, left as an asset until reversed and transferred in the proper accounting period.

**deferred credits**   accounts in the liability section of the balance sheet, representing revenues received but not earned until a future period.

**descending triangle**   a bullish sign involving flat support and declining resistance. As the breadth shrinks to a very narrow point, the expectation is for a reversal and uptrend to follow.

**diagonal spreads**   spreads opened with options on the same underlying stock with different strike prices and different expiration months.

**disruption risk**   the risk that trading in stocks may be disrupted by political or economic causes, acts of war, or natural disasters.

**distribution phase**   the third stage in a trend, in which leading investors or traders sell appreciated shares (uptrend) or buy depressed shares (downtrend), marking the end of the trend.

**diversification**   spreading of risk among several dissimilar stocks or other investments in order to avoid having a single risk event negatively affect the entire portfolio.

**dividend yield**   the return on dividends paid. To compute the annual dividend yield, divide annual dividends per share by the current price per share; the result is expressed as a percentage.

**dogs of the Dow**   a measurement of dividend yield and stock prices, based on the belief that the 10 DJIA stocks with the highest dividends relative to stock price are also likely to outperform the market average.

**doji**   a candlestick with little or no distance between opening and closing, so that a horizontal line is found instead of a rectangle.

**dollar cost averaging (DCA)**   a system of investing the same dollar amount into the market periodically regardless of price changes over time, on the theory that this reduces risk.

**double bottom**   a technical pattern consisting of two downward price spikes testing support. The failure to break through precedes a reversal and an uptrend after the double attempt.

**double top**   a technical pattern in which price rises to the resistance level twice without breaking through permanently; after this prices are expected to decline.

**Dow Jones Industrial Average (DJIA)**   a price-weighted average of 30 blue-chip industrial stocks, popularly used to judge the trend and strength or weakness of the stock market.

**Dow Theory**   a belief in trends set within the markets, based on the original beliefs and observations expressed by Charles Dow.

**downtrend**   in swing trading, a series of consecutive sessions with lower high prices and lower low prices in each session, compared to the previous session.

**dragonfly doji**   a bullish doji with a lower shadow only, recognizable by its formation of a capital letter T.

**earnings per share (EPS)**   the latest reported earnings, expressed as a division of earnings by the total shares outstanding during the reported year.

**Eastern technical indicators**   the analysis of charts to find price patterns and improve entry and exit of positions, based on the patterns revealed by candlesticks.

**effective tax rate**   the rate of taxes assessed on taxable income, combining both federal and state rates.

**efficient market theory (EMT)**   a belief that the price of stock reflects all known information about the company at all times, and changes rationally based on new information as it becomes available.

**engulfing pattern**   a two-session candlestick formation with the second day longer on both sides of the first day (engulfing its range). A bullish version consists of a black set-up day and a white second day; a bearish version consists of a white set-up and a black second day.

**enterprise value (EV)**   an alternative to the measurement of value based on equity alone, or market cap; EV includes all sources of capitalization, including holders of notes and bonds (debtors), as well as common and preferred stockholders.

**entry and exit signals**   indicators consisting of price patterns or changes, which traders use to improve the time of buy and sell decisions. These signals are meant to improve their chances of accurate timing to increase profits and reduce losses.

**equity funds**   mutual funds that create a portfolio from investments in stocks (equities) of listed companies.

**exchange-traded fund (ETF)**   a type of mutual fund with a pre identified basket of stocks with a common element. The ETF is traded over public exchanges just like shares of stock.

**ex-dividend date**   the cut-off date for earning of dividends. Stockholders who own stock before the close of the ex-date earn a dividend to be paid a few weeks later.

Anyone buying stock after the ex-date has to wait until the next quarter before earning dividends.

**exercise** the act by an owner of a call to buy shares at the fixed strike price, or by the owner of a put to sell shares at the fixed strike price.

**exhaustion gap** a gap occurring at the end of a trend, signifying a loss of momentum and a reversal in price direction.

**expiration date** the date when an option becomes worthless; the Saturday following the third Friday of the specified expiration month.

**exponential moving average (EMA)** a formula for weighted moving average, used to provide great impact to the latest entries on a stock price chart.

**extreme reaction risk** the risk that timing of buying or selling decisions will be based on overreaction to market conditions rather than made rationally or based on observed technical signals.

**extrinsic value** the portion of an option's premium beyond both intrinsic value and time value, reflecting the implied volatility of the option and varying based on time to expiration and proximity between current value of stock and strike price of the option. The price volatility of the underlying stock also directly impacts the extrinsic value of the option.

**failed signal** a technical signal indicating a price direction about to emerge (most notably a price reversal) that does not materialize or is contradicted in actual price movement.

**fair value** a fundamental indicator intended to value a stock and its growth potential based on a specific measurement; this is compared to the current market value of stock to seek bargain prices.

**family of funds** a group of funds offered by one mutual fund company but with different investment objectives.

**financial ratios** tests of related financial data including operating results for a period of time (usually one full year), or the working capital and capitalization status as of a specified date (usually year-end).

**financial statements** summaries of a company's operations for a defined period of time (one year or the latest quarter), and of the values of assets, liabilities, and equity accounts as of a specific date.

**fiscal year** the tax year used by a corporation, which may end in any quarter selected by the company. Fiscal years may correspond to the natural business cycle rather than to the calendar year.

**fixed-income funds** mutual funds that purchase bonds to generate interest income or stocks to yield higher-than-average dividends.

**forward P/E** a variation of the P/E ratio in which estimated earnings for the coming year are used in place of the latest reported actual earnings.

**front-end sales load** an alternative name for the load, so called because a sales commission is deducted from an investment before funds are used to buy mutual fund shares.

**fundamental analysis**  the study of financial statements and the trends revealed in the numbers, to identify a company's revenue and earnings history and capital strength. The purpose is to identify companies representing the best investment value.

**fundamental risk**  the risk that financial reports on which investors rely may not be accurate and might even mislead investors in extreme cases.

**gapping behavior**  differences in price levels between one day's closing price and the next day's opening price, especially when this incidence is repetitive or frequent.

**gaps**  spaces in trading found between one session's close and the next session's open.

**global fund**  a type of mutual fund investing in companies outside of the United States or based in the United States but serving an international market.

**gravestone doji**  a bearish doji with an upper shadow only, which looks like a capital T turned upside down.

**greed and panic risk**  the risk that buying will occur irrationally when prices are running up too far and too fast, or that selling will occur when prices are falling rapidly.

**gross profit**  the dollar value remaining when the cost of goods sold, or direct costs, is subtracted from revenue.

**growth stocks**  stocks of companies expected to report better-than-average earnings and to experience rapid stock price growth as a result, at least for the period in which the growth industry remains in an uptrend.

**hammer**  a candle with a small real body of either color, and a long lower shadow. It appears at the bottom of a downtrend and, if confirmed, indicates a bullish reversal.

**hanging man**  a candle with a small real body of either color, and a long lower shadow. It appears at the top of an uptrend and, if confirmed, indicates a bearish reversal.

**harami**  a two-candlestick pattern with a set-up day containing a higher high and a lower low. A bull harami consists of a black set-up followed by a white day, and a bear harami has a white set-up day followed by a black second day.

**head and shoulders**  a pattern in chart analysis consisting of three price spikes. The first and third (shoulders) are lower than the second (head). After the failed attempt at driving prices upward, price is expected to react by trending downward after the head and shoulders.

**hedge funds**  companies usually set up as private partnerships and with a limited number of high–net worth investors, specializing in high-return, high-risk leveraged market positions.

**horizontal spreads**  spreads opened with options on the same underlying stock with identical strike prices but different expiration months.

**implied volatility**  the level of volatility and risk in options trading, comparing current prices of options to established pricing models. The greater the gap between current market value and the pricing model price level, the higher the market volatility.

**in the money**  the status of an option when current value is higher than the call's strike or lower than the put's strike.

**income statement**   a financial statement summarizing revenue, costs, earnings, and profits for a specified period of time, usually a quarter or fiscal year.

**index funds**   mutual funds that invest in market-tracking indexes rather than directly in equity or debt positions.

**inflation risk**   the risk of losing purchasing power in money as a consequence of rising prices over time; for investors, inflation requires ever-higher returns on investment to offset the effects of inflation.

**insider trading**   the act of trading in the market based on information not available to the general public and provided by a source inside an organization or in a position to know news the general public does not have.

**institutional investors**   shareholders in publicly listed companies representing the majority of shares held, including mutual funds, pension programs, and insurance companies, as well as other concerns managing the investments of others.

**intangible assets**   assets lacking physical value, including goodwill and covenants not to compete.

**intra-day trading**   a variation of day trading, a strategy in which positions are opened and closed within single trading sessions or, at the most, two consecutive sessions.

**intrinsic value**   the portion of an option's premium when the current value of stock is higher than the call's strike or lower than the put's strike.

**investment club**   a group of individuals who pool their money together and share research, to select stocks for purchase over a period of time.

**investment strategy**   a set of rules and procedures an investor develops for picking the elements of a portfolio, identifying desired rates of return and risk levels, and determining when to sell.

**investor**   an individual most likely to select companies based on fundamental strength and to buy stock with the intention of holding it over many months or years.

**Japanese candlesticks**   alternative name for candlesticks and for the charts on which they are used.

**knowledge and experience risk**   the combined information you have gathered through research and observation, plus past investing and related activities; together, knowledge and experience ultimately determines how you view the markets and how you approach selection of stocks.

**large cap**   a classification of companies whose total equity value is greater than $10 billion.

**last trading day**   the final trading day for options, which is the trading day immediately before the third Saturday of the expiration month.

**leverage risk**   the risk resulting from borrowing money to invest. In the case of losses, leveraged positions not only have to be paid back, but losses have to be made up as well.

**line chart**   a simplified chart for tracking a stock's price, consisting of a single line connected between days, and normally reflecting the stock's closing price for each session.

**liquidity risk**   in the public exchanges, the possibility that high volume will curtail the availability of cash needed to complete trades in shares of stock.

**listed company**   a corporation whose shares are listed, quoted, and traded over a public exchange, with shares held publicly by either institutional or retail investors.

**load funds**   mutual funds that deduct a sales commission from all investments made, to be paid to a salesperson who recommends the investment.

**long candle**   a candle with an unusually long real body, either white or black, and likely to foreshadow reversal when it appears at the end of a trend.

**long position**   ownership of shares, accomplished by a buy order and involving the sequence buy-hold-sell.

**long-legged doji**   a doji with exceptionally long upper and lower shadows, with the small real body about halfway in the formation. This may be bullish or bearish depending on where it appears in the trend.

**long-term assets**   the net value (basis minus accumulated depreciation) of capital assets, including real estate, autos and trucks, machinery and equipment, furniture and furnishings, and tools.

**long-term liabilities**   all debts of a company owed beyond the next 12 months, including notes, contracts, and bonds.

**lost opportunity risk**   the risk that capital will be fully committed so that new investment opportunities cannot be taken, reducing future profits.

**lower shadow**   the vertical portion of a candlestick extending below the real body and representing a failed attempt during the session to move the price lower.

**MACD**   a popular technical indicator, meaning moving average convergence/divergence, the study of trends based on the proximity between price and averages.

**management fee**   the fee charged by a mutual fund to compensate its professional managers.

**margin account**   an account provided to investors by their brokers, allowing them to borrow up to one-half of the value of their portfolio.

**margin call**   a requirement that investors deposit additional funds to meet minimum margin requirements. If the margin call cannot be met, the broker will sell some or all of the portfolio assets.

**market capitalization**   the total dollar value of a company's net worth, including the most frequently used classifications of large cap, mid-cap, and small cap.

**market risk**   the risk that prices will decline, reducing the value of stocks, potentially for many months; market risk is the best-known and best-understood form of risk.

**marubozu**   a long candle, white or black, with no shadows or a shadow only above or only below the real body.

**mega-cap**   companies with equity value above $200 billion.

**micro-cap**   companies with equity value between $50 million and $300 million.

**mid-cap** a classification of companies whose total equity value is between $2 and $10 billion.

**minor trend** a price trend of only a few days, moving either upward or downward.

**momentum trading** a system of day trading based solely on identifying short-term trends and timing entry and exit based on the trend's strength or weakness (momentum).

**money market funds** mutual funds that buy only short-term money market instruments, and provide income but no growth to investors.

**mortgage pool** a type of pooled investment in which shares consist of part ownership in a pool of secured mortgage contracts.

**moving average (MA)** the average price over a fixed number of sessions, adjusted for each new session by removing the oldest and replacing it with the newest day, and then dividing the total by the total number of days.

**mutual fund** an investment company designed to combine the capital of many individuals to create a single portfolio designed to meet specified investment and risk objectives.

**naked call** alternative name for an uncovered call.

**narrow range day (NRD)** a trading session in which opening and closing prices are very close or identical, indicating exhaustion of the trend and a likely reversal about to occur.

**net asset value (NAV)** the day's ending value of a mutual fund, computed by adding the total asset value of the fund (minus any liabilities) and dividing the net total by the number of shares outstanding.

**net operating profit** the dollar value remaining when all expenses are deducted from gross profit.

**net profit** the "bottom line," the final profit when all adjustments and deductions have been made.

**net worth** the dollar value of a company's equity value (assets less liabilities), divided into capital stock and retained earnings (the sum of all profits and losses from year to year) and other equity adjustments.

**no-load funds** mutual funds that are purchased without deduction of a sales load, or commission.

**OHLC chart** a stock chart showing each session's trading range by way of a vertical stick, as well as opening and closing price noted by small horizontal sticks.

**open-end fund** a type of mutual fund that does not place limits on its number of subscribers or assets it manages.

**opening order** an order placed with a broker to create a position, either long or short.

**options** intangible contracts allowing their holders to control 100 shares of a specific stock for a fraction of the cost of trading those shares.

**oscillators** technical indicators that track price movement and identify overbought or oversold conditions. These aid in picking the best entry and exit points in trades.

**out of the money** the status of an option when current value is lower than the call's strike or higher than the put's strike.

**overdiversification** condition when a portfolio is spread so broadly that exceptional advantages in some holdings are offset by underperformance in others, resulting in a poor overall return.

**paper trading** a system of simulated investing in which a portfolio of cash can be used to buy shares of stock based on actual value in the current stock market. However, because it is a simulation, there is no risk. The purpose to paper trading is to demonstrate to a new investor how the markets work.

**pattern day trader** any trader who moves in and out of positions in the same stock four or more times within five consecutive trading sessions and who is required to maintain at least $25,000 in cash and securities in their brokerage account.

**percentage swing** price movement of a specified percentage below the high or above the low, used to generate entry or exit decisions as part of a swing trading strategy.

**political and economic risk** the risk that outside influences may affect stock valuation. Political changes, either domestic or international, may curtail activities or affect customers; economic activities may slow down production, prevent expansion, or prevent companies from hiring or retaining employees.

**preferred stock** classification of ownership with priority in dividend payments and liquidation above both debtors and common stockholders; however, preferred stockholders have no voting rights.

**premium** the value of an option. This is expressed as a numeral without a dollar sign and with two decimal places, denoting the value per share. A premium of 2.40, for example, means the option is priced at $240.

**prepaid assets** expenses paid in one year but properly assigned to two or more years, set up as an asset to be amortized properly to future periods.

**pretax profit** the net profit earned for a quarter or a fiscal year, before calculating the liability for income taxes; the net left when other income and expenses are added to or subtracted from net operating profit.

**price/earnings ratio (P/E)** a comparison between the current price per share and the latest reported earnings per share, indicating the current market perception of future earnings potential.

**price-weighted average** a kind of stock market average in which the prices of components are added together and divided by the number of stocks used; the result is that higher-priced stocks have more influence on the average than lower-priced stocks.

**primary trend** the overall direction of the market, either bullish or bearish, that lasts from a few months to several years.

**prospectus**  a disclosure document explaining the nature and risks of securities, including management and their compensation, investment objectives, and costs involved in buying shares.

**public participation phase**  the second phase of a trend, in which the market follows the lead of those in the accumulation phase and buys or sells shares in the indicated direction.

**pump and dump**  the purchase of shares and encouragement of others to do the same, hoping to drive prices higher and then sell at a profit.

**purchasing power**  the value of money when compared between years. As inflation rises, the dollar loses its purchasing power compared to past years.

**put**  an option providing its owner the right but not the obligation to sell 100 shares of a specified stock, at a fixed price, on or before a specified expiration date.

**random walk theory**  a theory stating that stock prices cannot be predicted using any fundamental or technical indicators, because price behavior is entirely random and unpredictable.

**range flip**  the observed change after a price breakout, in which previous resistance becomes new support in an uptrend, or in which previous support becomes new resistance in a downtrend.

**real body**  the middle rectangle of a candlestick, showing whether the session moved upward (white) or downward (black), and making it possible to spot trends immediately.

**Real Estate Investment Trust (REIT)**  a real estate investment conduit that trades on public exchanges like shares of stock.

**Real Estate Mortgage Investment Conduit (REMIC)**  a mortgage pool offered by a government-sponsored or government-guaranteed mortgage organization.

**record date**  the date on which recorded owners of stock earn a declared dividend even though payment does not take place until several weeks after; also called ex-dividend date.

**redemption fee**  a charge assessed by a mutual fund at the time shares are redeemed, not to exceed 2 percent of the redemption value.

**reinvested dividends**  those dividends used to automatically purchase additional shares of stock as opposed to taking payments in cash. Reinvested dividends earn the dividend yield at a compounded rate because future dividend payments are based on the total shares held, including shares purchased with quarterly dividends.

**Relative Strength Index (RSI)**  an oscillator that tracks upward and downward sessions and compares them to quantify momentum and provide an estimate of overbought or oversold conditions.

**resistance**  the highest price in a stock's trading range, or the high side of the price range at which both sides can agree to a trade.

**resistance zone**  a range of prices representing resistance, used in place of a single price.

**retail investors**    individuals who own shares in publicly traded companies through direct ownership (as opposed to buying shares in mutual funds).

**retained earnings**    the accumulated sum of a corporation's after-tax net profits, increased each year a profit is reported, and reduced whenever a net loss occurs.

**return on assets (ROA)**    a ratio comparing net return for a fiscal year, to total assets as of the end of that year. The purpose behind ROA is to calculate the effective investment in assets for the generation of profits.

**return on equity (ROE)**    a ratio comparing net return from operations to the value of shareholders' equity, used to measure the effective use of invested capital to generate profits.

**return on invested capital (ROIC)**    a ratio comparing net return adjusted for dividends paid, to total capital. This demonstrates how effectively a company uses its available resources to generate profits.

**reversal day**    the end of a trend; a session that moves in the direction opposite the established direction, signaling a high possibility of a reversal in the price direction.

**reverse head and shoulders**    a chart pattern involving three bottom price spikes. The first and third (reverse shoulders) are not as low as the second (the head). After the failed downward movement, prices are expected to reverse and trend upward.

**risk**    exposure to loss resulting from numerous market, economic, and company-specific causes.

**risk tolerance**    the degree of risk appropriate to each individual based on experience and knowledge, available capital, income, and willingness or unwillingness to take chances.

**rolling strategy**    closing a short option and replacing it with another option that expires later, with the intention of deferring or avoiding exercise.

**round-trip trade**    the complete steps involved with first opening and then closing a position.

**runaway gap**    a pattern of gapping action involving several sessions in close proximity, as part of a trend moving strongly in one direction without offsetting price movement.

**sales load**    a commission deducted from investments in mutual funds and paid to the salesperson.

**secondary market**    the government-sponsored market for purchasing of mortgage contracts from lenders, organizing them into larger mortgage pools and selling shares to investors.

**secondary trend**    a trend lasting from a few days to a few months, with prices moving counter to the direction of the primary trend.

**sector risk**    a risk identified with a particular sector and its industries, derived from business cycles, market conditions, or economic changes.

**sell to close/buy to close**    the type of closing order being placed. A sell to close is used to close an existing long position, and a buy to close is used to close an existing short position.

**set-up signals**   patterns or changes in price or volume that tell day traders and swing traders when likely trend reversals are about to take place.

**shadows**   the portion of a candlestick above or below the real body, representing the extent of trading range beyond opening and closing prices.

**shareholder service fees**   a mutual fund's charge for expenses of responding to client inquiries, either as part of a 12b-1 fee or separately from it.

**shares**   part ownership of a corporation that is listed publicly. Shares are bought and sold over public exchanges. Owners of shares are entitled to receive dividends and common stock owners are allowed to vote on matters of corporate management. Shares of stock rise and fall in value every day based on the ever-changing levels of supply and demand.

**short covering**   buying activity resulting from holders of shorted stock closing positions; when short covering occurs at a high volume, it may create an artificially high buy indicator.

**short position**   the sale of shares, accomplished with an opening sell order and involving the sequence sell-hold-buy.

**short position risk**   the risk incurred by selling as an opening step, in which traders hope for a price decline so the short position can be closed (bought), and the net difference will be a profit.

**short selling**   the act of borrowing stock and then selling it in the hope that the price will fall. If that occurs, shares can be closed by buying at a lower price. If the stock price rises, it creates a loss because the short position has to be closed (bought) at a higher price. Short sellers also have to pay interest on the shares borrowed to open the short position.

**small cap**   a classification of companies whose total equity value is less than $2 billion.

**specialty funds**   mutual funds that select portfolios based on a specific theme such as social consciousness.

**speculation**   short-term trading based on price movement in order to maximize profits based on immediate price movements and trends, distinguished from investment, which tends to involve longer-term hold periods.

**spinning top**   a candle with a small real body and long upper and lower shadows of about the same size; the spinning top is either bullish or bearish depending on where it is found.

**spreads**   option strategies combining two or more options on the same underlying stock, but with different strikes, or different expiration dates, or both.

**squeeze alert**   a series of three consecutive candle sessions. A bull squeeze alert consists of black candles, and a bear squeeze alert has three white candles. In both cases, each day's high is lower than the previous, and each day's low is higher than the previous.

**straddles**   option strategies involving opening of call and put positions with the same strike and expiration.

**strike** the fixed price of an option, at which the owner is allowed to trade 100 shares of stock.

**supply and demand** the economic forces that set prices for publicly traded stocks. When buyers want more shares than are immediately available from sellers, the excess demand drives up prices. When sellers want to sell more shares than buyers want to buy, the excess supply forces prices down. The interactive supply-and-demand forces are continuous.

**support** the lowest price in a stock's trading range, or the low side of the price range at which sellers and buyers are able to agree on price.

**support zone** a range of prices representing support, used in place of a single price.

**swing trading** a short-term trading strategy based on recognition of trends lasting only a few days (usually three to five), with entry and exit based on set-up signals.

**synthetic position** an option position involving two or more open contracts designed to act in the same manner as another security, such as stock.

**tails** alternative name for a candlestick's shadows, especially when longer than average.

**tangible book value** the net capital value of a company (assets minus liabilities) further reduced for all intangible assets. When the tangible value is divided by outstanding shares of stock, the result is the tangible book value per share.

**tax risk** the risk that after-tax return on investment will fall short of the return needed to preserve spending power after inflation.

**tax-free bond funds** mutual funds that invest solely in municipal bonds that offer tax-free interest to investors.

**technical analysis** the study of price patterns, charts, and trends to time entry and exit into positions in stock, compared to fundamental analysis, which studies trends to pick companies.

**technical knowledge and experience risk** the risk that a range of technical indicators is difficult to explain without a background in interpreting them and recognizing their significance and effect on price trends.

**technical risk** any risk directly involving price, reflected in price volatility and trends as well as in related indicators such as trading volume.

**terms** the four attributes of every option that cannot be changed or replaced: type of option (call or put), strike, expiration date, and underlying security.

**three black crows** a bearish candlestick formation of three consecutive sessions. All three are black. Each day's closing price is lower than the preceding close and each day's opening price is lower than the previous day's open.

**three white soldiers** a bullish candlestick formation of three consecutive sessions. All three are white. Each day's closing price is higher than the preceding close and each day's opening price is higher than the previous day's open.

**time value** the portion of an option's premium that varies with time remaining to expiration; the further away expiration date, the higher the time value. This value declines gradually until the last two months, when time value falls rapidly, ending at zero on expiration day.

**total capitalization** the combination of long-term debt (debt capitalization) and net worth (equity capitalization).

**trader** an individual who buys and sells stock based on short-term price trends, who is focused on stock price changes rather than on the financial history of the company.

**trading halt** the temporary suspension of trading in a particular security in anticipation of an imbalance that may be created by upcoming announcements of mergers or acquisitions, or negotiations between companies.

**trading range** the distance between recent high and low price levels; the price area in which buyers and sellers currently interact with one another.

**trend** the established direction or movement of price, or changes in an indicator, that define a company's value over many months or years.

**trend line** a straight line drawn beneath a rising support level or above a falling resistance level. Once price levels reverse and interrupt the line, a reversal may be indicated or confirmed.

**triangle** a trend involving changes in the breadth of the trading range. As the range narrows during the current trend direction, the likelihood of reversal increases.

**true range** a recalculated trading range including not only a single session, but the range between one session's closing price and the next session's high.

**uncovered call** a short call written when the trader does not also own 100 shares of the underlying stock; a high-risk option strategy.

**underdiversification** a common condition in which a portfolio is focused on too few stocks or on stocks exposed to the same market risks.

**underlying security** the stock or other security controlled by the option. In the case of options on stock, every option contract controls 100 shares of the underlying security.

**unit investment trust (UIT)** a fund that purchases income-generating securities (bonds and stocks) and creates a trust in which shares are sold to investors. Periodic payments are made for interest, dividends, and capital gains earned throughout the life of the UIT.

**upper shadow** the vertical portion of a candlestick extending above the real body and representing a failed attempt during the session to move the price higher.

**uptrend** in swing trading, a series of consecutive sessions with higher high prices and higher low prices in each session, compared to the previous session.

**value investing** a method for picking long-term investments by determining their true value and quality, and then seeking discounted prices to find bargains.

**variable annuity** a product similar to a mutual fund, which combines investment dollars from many individuals to create a portfolio. The issuing company agrees to make a series of payments in future years based on the value of contributed capital and performance of the securities in the portfolio.

**vertical spreads** spreads opened with options on the same underlying stock with identical expiration dates but different strike prices.

**volatility** the degree of price change within a defined period of time, used as a measurement of market risk in a particular stock.

**volatility risk** a technical variation on the broader market risk, involving the degree of exposure traders accept in picking and timing positions in stock.

**volume** the level of trading in a stock, represented by the number of shares exchanged between buyers and sellers in a specified period of time (a trading day, for example).

**volume spike** a single trading session with higher-than-average volume, signaling the possibility of a coming reversal of price movement.

**Western technical indicators** the traditional technical patterns and developments used in technical analysis to time entry and exit from trading positions.

**wicks** alternative name for a candlestick's shadows.

**working capital** the cash available to the organization to pay current obligations and to fund future growth and pay dividends; a fundamental test of money management.

**writer** a trader who opens, or writes, a short position in options.

# About the Author

**Michael C. Thomsett** (www.MichaelThomsett.com) has written more than 70 books on investing, real estate, business, and management. He is author of several Wiley books, including the eight editions of the bestselling *Getting Started in Options*, as well as *Getting Started in Fundamental Analysis, Getting Started in Real Estate Investing,* and *Getting Started in Swing Trading.* He also has written numerous other stock investing and trading books, including *Winning with Stocks* (Amacom Books), *Stock Profits* (FT Press), and *Mastering Fundamental Analysis* and *Mastering Technical Analysis* (Dearborn Press). The author contributes regularly to many web sites, including Minyanville Media, and writes articles for the *AAII Journal* and NAIC's *Better Investing.* He also writes a weekly investing and trading blog (www.ftpress.com/blogs/). Thomsett has been writing professionally since 1978 and full time since 1985. He lives near Nashville, Tennessee.

# Index